Children's COOKBOOK

LONDON, NEW YORK, MUNICH,
MELBOURNE, AND DELHI

Project Editor Catherine Saunders
U.S. Editors Madeline Farbman and Christine Heilman
Designer Lisa Crowe
Home Economist and Food Stylist Katharine Ibbs
Design Assistants Lynne Moulding and Justin Greenwood
Assistant Home Economists Lisa Harrison, Sarah Tildesley, Fergal Connolly
Consultant Nicola Graimes
Publishing Manager Cynthia O'Neill Collins
Art Director Mark Richards
Category Publisher Alex Kirkham
Production Rochelle Talary
DTP Designer Dean Scholey

First American Edition, 2004
05 06 07 08 10 9 8 7 6 5 4 3

Published in the United States by
DK Publishing, Inc.
375 Hudson Street
New York, New York 10014

Published in Great Britain by Dorling Kindersley Limited.

A catalog record for this book is available from the Library of Congress.

ISBN 0-7566-0597-0

Reproduced by in Singapore by Colourscan
Printed and bound in China by Toppan

Acknowledgments
The publisher would like to thank the photographer's assistant Michael Hart, especially for the endless cups of tea!
A big thank-you to all the young chefs who acted as hand models—Latoya Bailey, Hannah Broom, Natika Clarke,
Hannah Leaman, Toby Leaman, Rozina McHugh, Louis Moorcraft, Lily Sansford, Sadie Sansford, Gabriella Soper,
Olivia Sullivan-Davis, James Tilley, and Hope Wadman.

Discover more at
www.dk.com

Children's COOKBOOK

Recipes by Katharine Ibbs
Photography by Howard Shooter

Contents

p.12-13

p.42-43

p.70-71

★ Desserts

p.86-87

★ Baking

p.110-111

p.72-73

p.80-81

Introduction

Whether you want to learn how to cook or are already a budding chef, this is the book for you!

Cooking is fun, and this book introduces you to key cooking techniques—from mashing to marinating, boiling to baking. And with over 50 tasty recipes to choose from, there's something for everyone!

Eating a healthy diet

It's important to take care of your body so that you feel healthy and happy. One of the best ways to do this is to eat a balanced diet. This means that your meals should contain a balance of the main food groups—protein, carbohydrates, fiber, fat, and vitamins and minerals.

★ Protein

This helps you grow. It also builds up your muscles and helps your body work correctly. Meat, fish, dairy products (such as milk, eggs, and cheese), legumes (such as peas, beans, and lentils), and nuts are good sources of protein.

★ Carbohydrates

These give you energy so that you can grow and lead an active life. Potatoes, cereals (such as wheat, which is used to make bread and pasta), grains (such as rice and oats), and legumes (such as peas, beans, and lentils) are good sources of carbohydrates.

★ Fiber

Your body needs fiber to help keep your intestines healthy and to prevent constipation. Cereals (such as whole-wheat bread), legumes (such as peas, beans, and lentils), and fruits and vegetables with their skin on (such as apples and potatoes) all contain fiber.

★ Fat

Although too much of it is bad for you, fat is still an important nutrient. It is a good source of energy and helps your body absorb some vitamins. The best kinds of fat are polyunsaturated and monounsaturated. Foods that contain these are oily fish (such as tuna and salmon), avocados, nuts, seeds and oils (such as olive oil, sunflower oil, and vegetable oil).

★ Vitamins and minerals

If you eat a healthy diet, you should get all the vitamins and minerals that you need. Vitamins help your body work properly and minerals help your body grow and repair itself which is important for healthy skin, bones, and teeth. As well as three well-balanced meals every day, you should eat plenty of fresh fruit and vegetables because they are excellent sources of vitamins and minerals.

How to use the recipes

Every page is packed full of information about cooking techniques, healthy eating, and staying safe in the kitchen. Each recipe has an easy-to-follow design, which is explained below. So relax, have fun, and GET COOKING!

Difficulty ratings help you to pick the most suitable recipes.
1 = easy
2 = medium
3 = hard

Estimated preparation and cooking times help you plan your meals.

A tool checklist helps you gather everything you need before you start cooking.

Techniques that appear in the glossary are highlighted in the recipes and at the top of the page.

The ingredients are pictured to help you find them, but remember, they do not show the exact quantities!

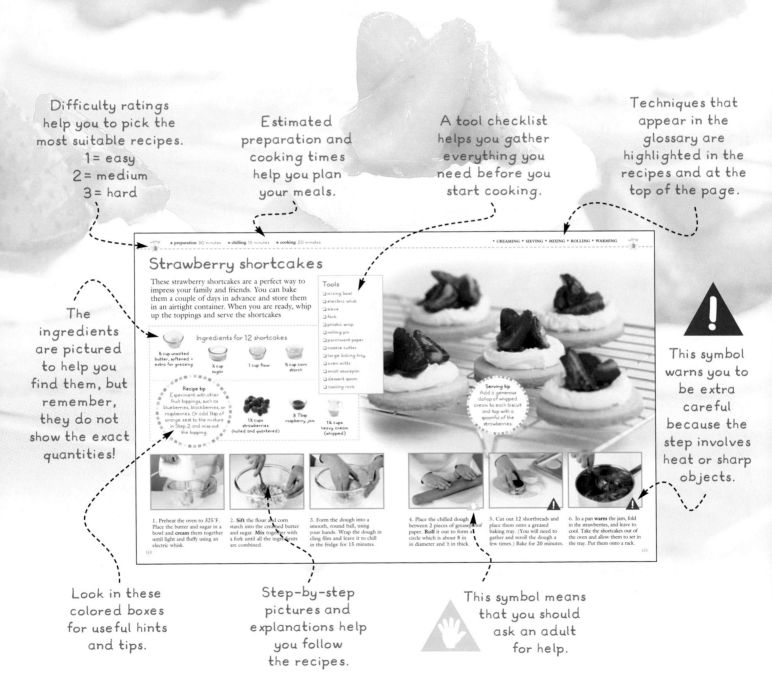

● preparation 30 minutes ● chilling 15 minutes ● cooking 20 minutes ● CREAMING ● SIEVING ● MIXING ● ROLLING ● WARMING

Strawberry shortcakes

These strawberry shortcakes are a perfect way to impress your family and friends. You can bake them a couple of days in advance and store them in an airtight container. When you are ready, whip up the toppings and serve the shortcakes

Ingredients for 12 shortcakes

½ cup unsalted butter, softened + extra for greasing

¼ cup sugar

1 cup flour

¼ cup corn starch

Recipe tip
Experiment with other fruit toppings, such as blueberries, blackberries, or raspberries. Or add 1tsp of orange zest to the mixture in Step 2 and miss out the topping.

1¼ cups strawberries (hulled and quartered)

3 Tbsp raspberry jam

1¼ cups heavy cream (whipped)

Tools
☐ mixing bowl
☐ electric whisk
☐ sieve
☐ fork
☐ plastic wrap
☐ rolling pin
☐ parchment paper
☐ cookie cutter
☐ large baking tray
☐ oven mitts
☐ small saucepan
☐ dessert spoon
☐ cooling rack

Serving tip
Add a generous dollop of whipped cream to each biscuit and top with a spoonful of the strawberries.

1. Preheat the oven to 325°F. Place the butter and sugar in a bowl and **cream** them together until light and fluffy using an electric whisk.

2. **Sift** the flour and corn starch into the creamed butter and sugar. **Mix** together with a fork until all the ingredients are combined.

3. Form the dough into a smooth, round ball, using your hands. Wrap the dough in cling film and leave it to chill in the fridge for 15 minutes.

4. Place the chilled dough between 2 pieces of greaseproof paper. **Roll** it out to form a circle which is about 8 in in diameter and ½ in thick.

5. Cut out 12 shortbreads and place them onto a greased baking tray. (You will need to gather and reroll the dough a few times.) Bake for 20 minutes.

6. In a pan **warm** the jam, fold in the strawberries, and leave to cool. Take the shortcakes out of the oven and allow them to set in the tray. Put them onto a rack.

This symbol warns you to be extra careful because the step involves heat or sharp objects.

Look in these colored boxes for useful hints and tips.

Step-by-step pictures and explanations help you follow the recipes.

This symbol means that you should ask an adult for help.

Cooking rules

These recipes have been specially created to help you learn both basic cooking skills and more advanced techniques. Follow these simple guidelines for fun, safe, and successful cooking.

★ Golden rules

1. Be safe—always be extra careful when you see this symbol, and especially when using sharp knives or hot stoves and ovens.
2. Be sensible—ask an adult for help and advice if you need it, especially when you see this symbol.
3. Be clean—always wash your hands before you start cooking, tie back long hair, and wear an apron to protect your clothes.
4. Be prepared—always read the recipe thoroughly and gather all your ingredients and tools before starting to cook.
5. Be consistent—when following a recipe, use standard measuring cups and spoons. All teaspoon and tablespoon measurements should be level, not heaped.

★ Hygiene rules

1. Wash all fruits and vegetables, and always use separate cutting boards for meat and vegetables.
2. Don't spread germs—always wash your hands thoroughly, especially after touching raw meat or fish.
3. Clean up as you go, and make sure that you have a sponge or dishcloth handy to wipe up any spills or messes.
4. Store cooked and raw food separately.
5. Keep meat and fish in the refrigerator until needed, and be sure they are cooked properly.
6. Always check the sell-by and use-by dates on all ingredients.

★ Heat rules

1. Always use oven mitts when handling hot pans, trays, and bowls.
2. Don't put hot things directly onto the work surface; always use a trivet, mat, or sturdy wooden board.
3. When cooking on the stove, turn pot handles to the side (away from the heat) so that you are less likely to bump them.
4. When you are stirring food on the stove, grip the handle firmly to steady the pan.

★ Chef's rules

1. Be creative—cooking is supposed to be fun, so relax and don't be scared to adapt the recipes to suit your personal tastes.
2. Be confident—cooking is about trying new things. Just go for it and cook up a storm!
3. Be calm—take your time, and don't panic if the food doesn't turn out quite as you hoped. Most likely it will still taste great, or you will have learned a valuable lesson for next time!
4. Vary your meals—don't eat the same thing all the time. A balanced diet means that you should eat different types of food.

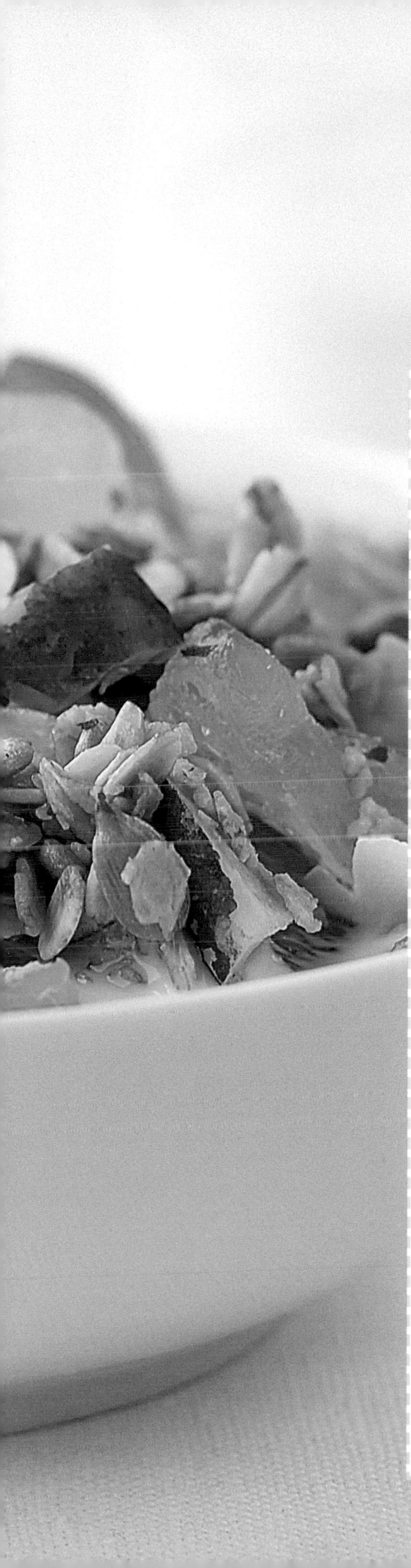

Breakfast

After a good night's sleep, your body will be running low on energy and essential nutrients. Eating a good breakfast will wake you up and get you ready to face the day's challenges. Whether it's a tough day at school, where you need to concentrate, or a fun-filled weekend, where you'll be constantly active, it's very important to start your day the right way.

The best foods to eat for breakfast are those that are high in fiber and carbohydrates. Good foods for this are whole-wheat bread, cereal, and oats because they slowly release energy throughout the day. Fresh fruit is also great because it gives you a healthy burst of vitamins to start the day. An egg-based breakfast will provide you with protein to build and repair your body.

easy 1 • **preparation** 5-10 minutes • **cooking** none

Fruit smoothie

Smoothies are easy to make and taste delicious at any time of day. Follow these four simple steps for a burst of fruity goodness.

Ingredients for 2-4 servings

1 cup ripe strawberries

1 ripe banana

1 cup milk

1 Tbsp honey (optional)

½ cup plain yogurt

Recipe idea

Replace the banana and strawberries with a large mango and half a medium melon, and use ½ cup orange juice and 1 Tbsp lime juice instead of milk.

Tools

- ❑ sharp knife
- ❑ cutting board
- ❑ blender
- ❑ measuring spoons

1. Rinse and drain the strawberries in cold water and then **hull** them by holding the pointed end and slicing off the stem.

2. Cut the strawberries in half and put them to one side. Peel the banana and throw away the skin. **Slice** the banana, for easy blending in Step 4.

3. Carefully put the banana and strawberries into the blender. Add the milk, yogurt, and honey and put the lid on securely.

4. **Blend** the mixture until it is completely smooth. Pour the smoothie into glasses and enjoy—what a great way to start the day!

Chef's tip
For an ice-cold summer treat, add a scoop or two of ice cream to the smoothie mixture in Step 3.

easy 1 • **preparation** 5 minutes • **cooking** 5-10 minutes

Boiled eggs

Eggs can be cooked in a variety of different ways and are an excellent source of protein. The simplest method is to boil them for a delicious and nutritious breakfast. The most important thing to remember when boiling eggs is timing, because this makes the difference between a soft-boiled egg and a hard-boiled egg.

1. Half-fill a small saucepan with water and place it on the stove. Gently lower the eggs into the pan and bring the water to a boil.

Ingredients for 2 servings

2 eggs

To serve

2 slices of whole-wheat bread

butter or margarine

Tools

- ❑ small saucepan
- ❑ slotted spoon
- ❑ toaster
- ❑ bowl of cold water
- ❑ 2 egg cups
- ❑ teaspoon

2. **Boil** the eggs for 4 minutes. While the eggs are cooking, you can make the toast. Place the bread in the toaster and toast until golden brown.

3. Remove the eggs with a slotted spoon and briefly dip them in cold water. This will cool the eggs and prevent them from cooking any further.

4. Place each egg in an egg cup and tap the top with the back of a teaspoon. Carefully slice off the top with the spoon. Serve with strips of buttered toast.

Food fact
Although the yolk of your soft-boiled egg will be runny, a properly cooked egg should always have a firm egg white. If the white of your egg is still runny, it hasn't been cooked for long enough!

Chef's tip
For hard-boiled eggs, boil the eggs for 6–7 minutes and make sure that they cool completely in Step 3.

medium 2 • **preparation** 10 minutes • **cooking** 15 minutes

Granola

This breakfast recipe is definitely worth getting out of bed for! Create a homemade cereal full of important fiber and carbohydrates with a tasty combination of oats, fruit, nuts, and seeds.

Tools

- ❑ medium saucepan
- ❑ wooden spoon
- ❑ sharp knife
- ❑ nonstick baking tray
- ❑ large mixing bowl
- ❑ cutting board
- ❑ plate
- ❑ measuring spoons
- ❑ oven mitts

Ingredients for 6 servings

1 Tbsp olive oil

3 Tbsp honey

2 cups jumbo rolled oats

½ cup brazil nuts (optional)

¼ cup sunflower seeds

½ cup dried pineapple pieces

½ cup dried banana chips

½ cup dried apricots

½ cup toasted coconut flakes (optional)

Recipe idea

Try other dried fruits, nuts, or seeds. Raisins, tropical fruits, hazelnuts, or pumpkin seeds would all taste great in this recipe!

To serve

one of the following

milk

plain or flavored yogurt

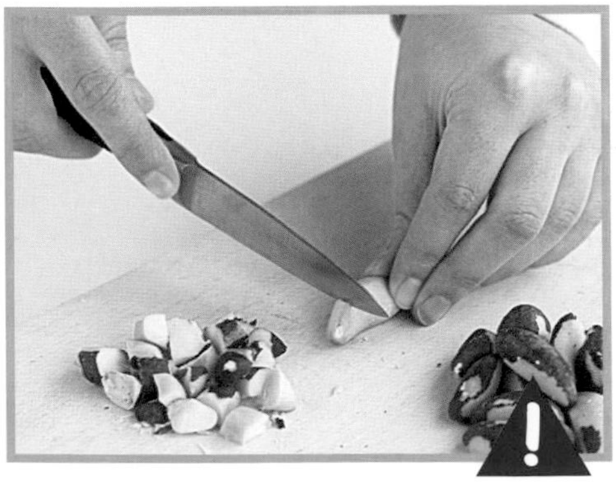

1. **Chop** the brazil nuts into medium-sized pieces. Remember, if you are allergic to nuts or do not like them, you should skip this step.

2. Preheat the oven to 400°F. Pour the oil and honey into the saucepan. Gently warm them over a low heat until they melt together.

3. Make sure the heat has been turned off and then pour the oats, nuts, and sunflower seeds into the melted syrup mixture. Stir until well coated.

This cereal will stay fresh and yummy for up to two weeks if you store it an airtight container.

Serving tip
Serve your cereal in a bowl with milk or a dollop of your favorite yogurt.

4. Tip the oat mixture on to a baking tray. Put it in the preheated oven for 10 minutes, or until the edges turn golden. The oats should form clusters.

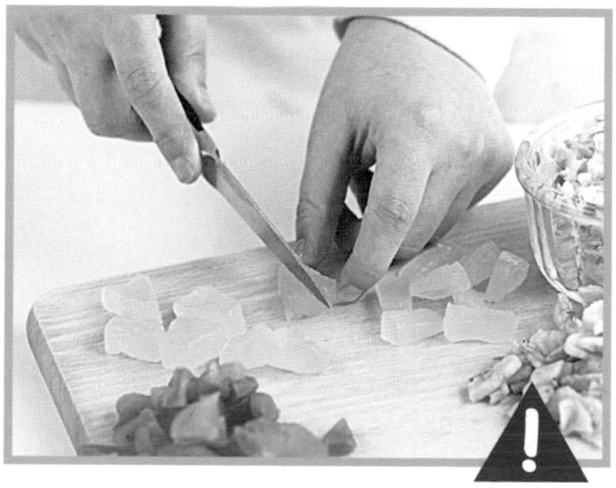

5. Cut the pineapple chunks in half, quarter the apricots, and break the banana chips into small pieces. **Mix** all the fruit and coconut together in a bowl.

6. Spoon the oat clusters onto a plate and leave them to cool for a few minutes. Add the oat clusters to the bowl of fruit and coconut and mix them together.

medium 2 • **preparation** 5 minutes • **cooking** 5 minutes

Scrambled eggs

Get cracking with this great breakfast idea! The secret of scrambled eggs is not to overcook them in Step 4; otherwise, they will become dry and rubbery.

Ingredients for 1 serving

2 eggs

1 Tbsp milk

salt and pepper

a pat of unsalted butter

To serve

1 slice of bread (toasted)

butter or margarine

ketchup

Tools

- ❑ mixing bowl
- ❑ whisk
- ❑ medium pan
- ❑ wooden spoon

1. To **crack** an egg, tap it on the side of a bowl and gently pull the shell apart so that the insides drop into the bowl. Repeat with the other egg.

See p.125 for expert tips on how to crack an egg like this!

2. Add the milk to the bowl of eggs. Season with salt and pepper and **whisk** all the ingredients together until they are mixed completely.

3. Over low heat, gently melt the butter in the pan. You must be very careful when doing this because if the pan gets too hot, the butter will spit.

4. Carefully pour the beaten egg mixture into the pan and stir constantly for 2–3 minutes. The eggs will become firm but should still look moist.

Serving tip
Scrambled eggs taste great on lightly buttered toast, with a dollop of ketchup!

hard 3 • **preparation** 10 minutes • **cooking** 15 minutes

Breakfast omelet

This omelet has just the right ingredients—eggs, bacon, tomatoes, and mushrooms—to give you all the protein and vitamins you need to start the day. Serve it as a filling weekend brunch, or with a salad as a lunch or light meal.

The omelet should be firm but still moist when it is cooked in Step 6.

Tools

- ❑ whisk
- ❑ measuring cup
- ❑ grater
- ❑ wooden spoon
- ❑ sharp knife
- ❑ 2 cutting boards
- ❑ small nonstick frying pan or omelet pan
- ❑ wooden spatula
- ❑ 2 plates
- ❑ paper towels

Ingredients for 1 omelet

2 eggs

2 Tbsp milk

⅓ cup cheddar cheese

a pat of unsalted butter

salt and pepper

For the filling

2 strips bacon

1 tsp sunflower oil

1 cup mushrooms

1 tomato

Recipe idea
Experiment with other fillings, such as onions, zucchini, peppers, or even different kinds of cheese!

Serving tip
A dollop of ketchup or slice of hot buttered toast would taste great with this omelet.

1. **Whisk** the eggs and milk together in a measuring cup (to make it easy to pour in Step 5.) **Grate** the cheese and stir it into the egg mixture. Season.

2. Cut the tomato into small chunks and thinly **slice** the mushrooms. On a separate cutting board, cut the bacon into cubes.

3. Place the frying pan over medium heat and **fry** the bacon for 3 minutes or until crisp. Put the bacon on a plate lined with paper towels.

4. Heat the oil and fry the mushrooms for 2 minutes. Add the tomato and cook for 1 minute. Put the tomato and mushrooms onto the plate.

5. Melt the butter in the pan. Pour in the egg so that it covers the base of the pan. Cook the egg over medium heat until the edges begin to cook and set.

6. Using a spatula, push the cooked egg into the center of the pan. The uncooked egg will run to the sides. Repeat until all the egg is cooked.

7. Shake the pan to release the omelet and spoon the filling over one half. Slide the omelet out onto a plate and gently flip the unfilled half over the top.

• **preparation** 10 minutes • **standing** 30 minutes (optional) • **cooking** 20 minutes

Blueberry pancakes

Making batter is a useful skill, and the small size makes these pancakes perfect for first-time flippers! Here's a handy tip: if you leave the batter to stand for half an hour before adding the fruit and cooking it, it has a lighter texture.

Tools

- ❑ sieve
- ❑ mixing bowl
- ❑ wooden spoon
- ❑ whisk
- ❑ measuring cup
- ❑ large frying pan
- ❑ serving spoon
- ❑ dessert spoon
- ❑ spatula

Ingredients for 8 pancakes

1¼ cups flour

1 tsp baking powder

2–3 pinches of salt

⅔ cup milk

1 egg

¼ cup sugar

1 cup fresh blueberries

2 Tbsp unsalted butter

To serve (optional)

1 large banana (peeled and sliced)

maple syrup

Recipe idea

The blueberries can be replaced with 1 large banana (chopped) in Step 3. You could even try plain pancakes, served with butter and jam, or just some maple syrup.

1. **Sift** the flour, baking powder, and salt into a mixing bowl. Stir in the sugar with a wooden spoon and set the bowl aside.

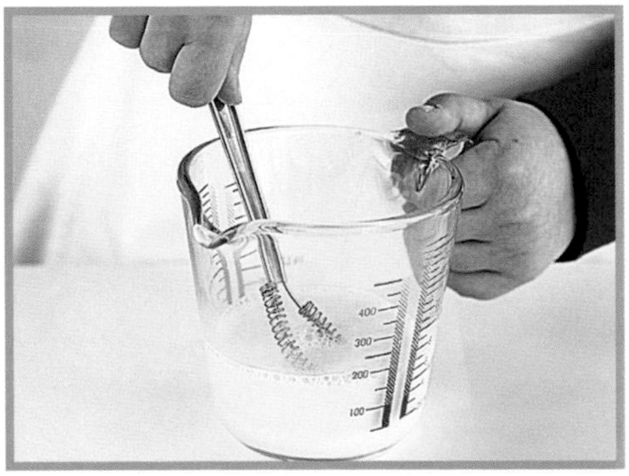

2. **Crack** the egg into a bowl, add it to the milk, and **whisk** them together. Do this in a measuring cup so the mixture can be poured easily in Step 3.

3. Pour the milk and egg mixture into the flour and **beat** with a wooden spoon. Gently **fold** in the blueberries, being careful not to crush them.

See p. 123–125 for tips on the techniques used in this recipe.

Serving tip
These pancakes taste great served with slices of banana and some maple syrup.

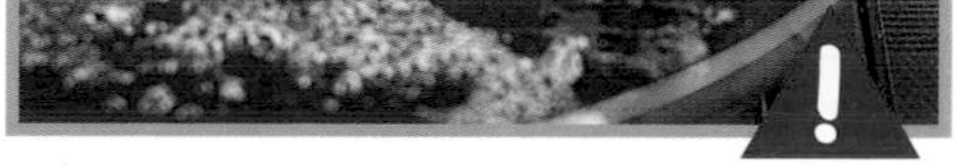

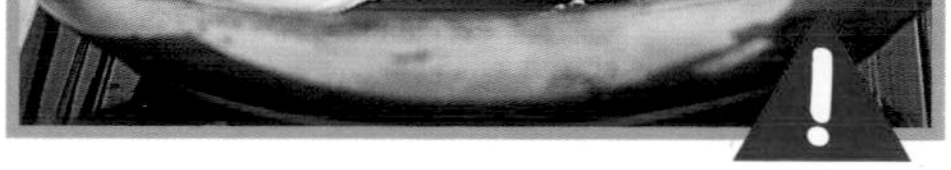

4. Over medium heat, melt a quarter of the butter in a large frying pan. When the butter begins to bubble, you are ready to start cooking!

5. Ladle two spoonfuls of batter into the frying pan. **Fry** the pancakes for 2 minutes or until bubbles appear on top and the undersides turn golden.

6. Use a spatula to flip the cakes and cook the other side for 2 minutes or until the cakes are cooked through. Repeat with the rest of the batter.

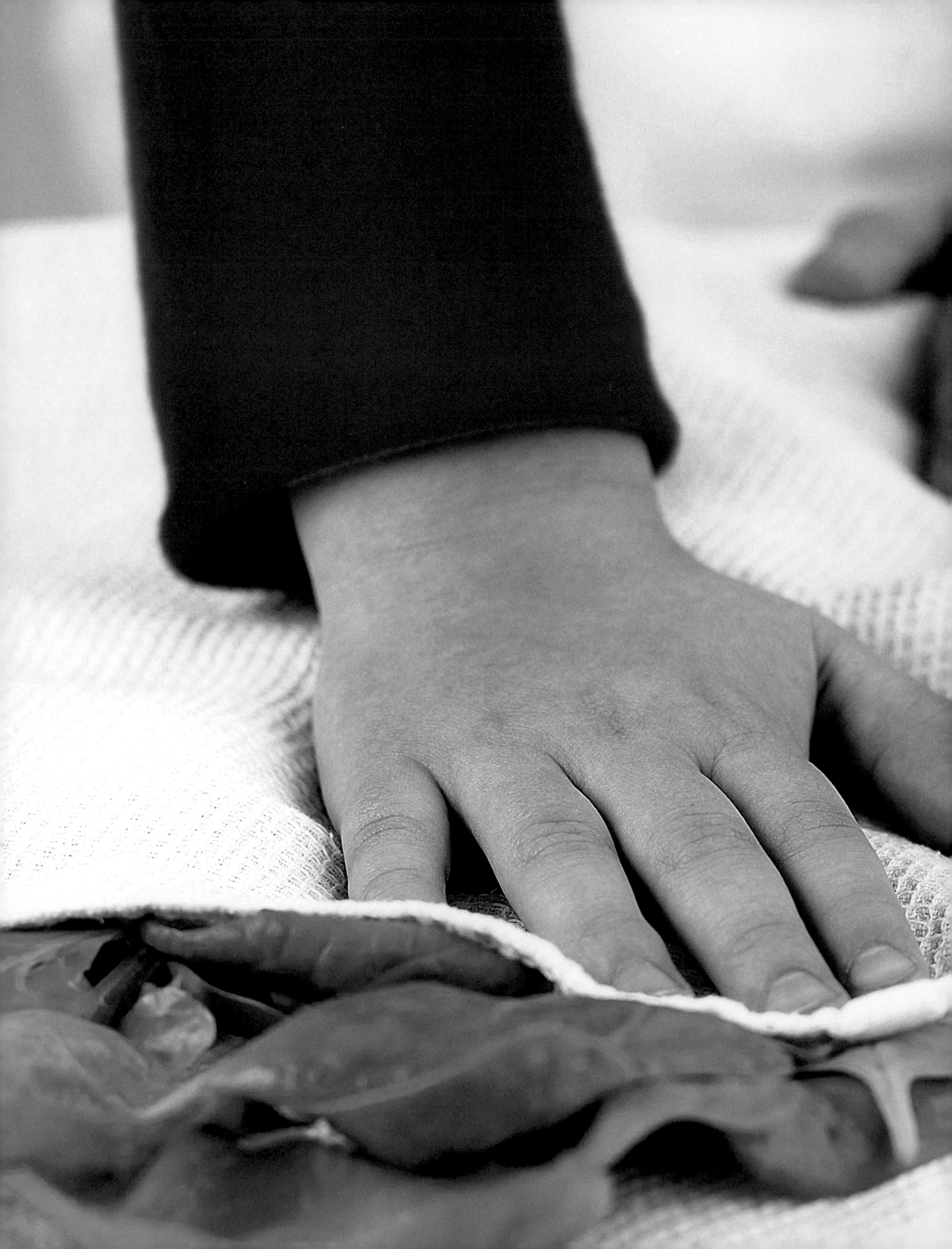

Light meals

This section introduces some great ideas for tasty lunches and light meals. Every meal you eat should have a healthy balance of essential nutrients. If you are eating in the middle of the day, it's very important to eat the kinds of food that will satisfy your hunger and give you energy but won't make you too full to have any fun in the afternoon!

You will also learn some important new skills and techniques in this section, from slicing and dicing to marinating and broiling. Remember to refer to the glossary on p.122–125 for extra tips!

easy 1 • **preparation** 15 minutes • **cooking** none

Green salad with dressing

Salad is delicious as a light meal or snack and can also be served as a nutritious accompaniment to a main meal.

Ingredients for 4–6 servings

3 cups mixed salad greens, e.g., lettuce, spinach, watercress

half large cucumber (diced)

12–18 cherry tomatoes (halved)

For the dressing

3 Tbsp olive oil

1 Tbsp fresh lemon juice

salt and pepper

1 tsp wholegrain mustard

1 tsp honey

Tools

- ❑ teaspoon
- ❑ jar with secure lid
- ❑ colander
- ❑ clean dish towel
- ❑ large mixing bowl

1. Spoon all the dressing ingredients into a clean jar and put the lid on tightly. Shake the jar to **mix** the ingredients together.

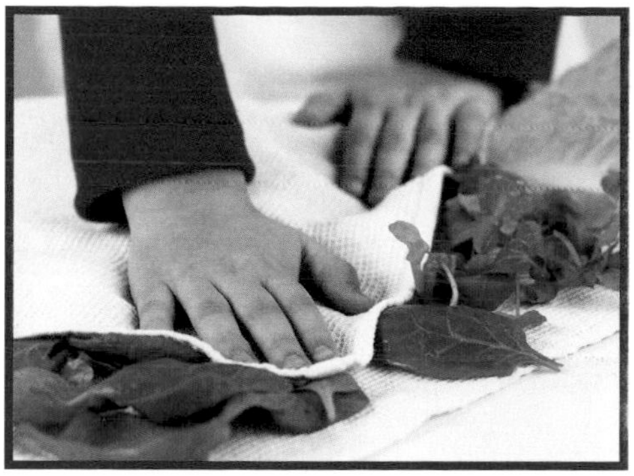

2. Rinse and drain the salad greens using a colander. Put them on a clean dish towel and gently pat dry. Tear the leaves into smaller pieces.

3. Using your hands, carefully mix the salad greens, cucumber, and tomatoes together in a large bowl. Transfer the mixed salad into individual bowls.

4. Shake the dressing again and **drizzle** some over each bowl of salad. Leave the jar of dressing on the side so that you can add more if you like.

Serving tip
Always dress the salad just before you eat, so that it does not turn soggy!

Try adding other ingredients to your salad, such as olives, onions, nuts, cheese, or croûtons (see p.32–33).

Baked potatoes

Here's a great tip: if you like the skin of your baked potato to be firm, roll the potato in a little olive oil after scrubbing it in Step 1.

1. Preheat the oven to 400°F. Scrub the potatoes in cold water, and pat them dry. Prick the potatoes all over with a fork.

Ingredients for 2 servings

2 large baking potatoes

For the filling

2 Tbsp sour cream

butter (optional)

1 cup broccoli florets (cut into tiny pieces)

1 cup cheddar cheese (grated)

pepper

Recipe idea

Try other toppings, such as crumbled, fried bacon or experiment with other types of cheese. You could even serve them plain, with just butter, salt, and pepper.

Tools

- ❑ fork
- ❑ cutting board
- ❑ sharp knife
- ❑ paper towels
- ❑ mixing bowl
- ❑ dessert spoon
- ❑ saucepan
- ❑ colander
- ❑ roasting pan/baking tray

2. **Bake** the potatoes for 1–1½ hours or until they are soft in the center. Carefully remove the potatoes from the oven and cut a cross in the top of each.

3. While the potatoes are baking, boil the broccoli for 4 minutes. Drain the broccoli and **mix** it with the cheese and sour cream. Season with pepper.

4. Using paper towels to protect your hands, squeeze the bottom corners of each potato to open it up. Watch out—the potatoes will still be very hot!

When the potato is cooked, it will be soft in the middle. Use a knife or skewer to check this.

Serving tip
Spread a little butter on your potato and spoon on the filling. It will all melt and taste yummy!

Dips and dippers

These recipes make great snacks, but they can also be served with some of the other recipes. For example, potato wedges taste great with the burgers on p.40–41, and guacamole goes well with the chicken wraps on p.54–55.

Tools

- ❑ kitchen scissors
- ❑ 2 nonstick baking trays
- ❑ oven mitts
- ❑ pastry brush
- ❑ sharp knife
- ❑ cutting board
- ❑ roasting pan
- ❑ food processor
- ❑ dessert spoon
- ❑ mixing bowl

Ingredients for 6–8 servings

potato wedges

4 small baking potatoes

2 Tbsp olive oil

1 tsp ground paprika

salt and pepper

guacamole

3 ripe avocados

½ red onion (finely chopped)

1 garlic clove (crushed)

2 tomatoes (deseeded and chopped)

juice of 1 lime

salt and pepper

2–3 sprigs chopped fresh cilantro (optional)

3–4 dashes hot sauce (optional)

hummus

15-oz can chickpeas

3 Tbsp olive oil

½ tsp ground cumin

2 Tbsp tahini paste

1 garlic clove (chopped)

juice of ½ lemon

tortilla chips

4 flour tortillas

salt and pepper

2 Tbsp unsalted butter (melted)

Chef's tip
Season the hummus with salt and pepper and sprinkle with a little paprika for decoration!

1. Preheat the oven to 350°F. Cut the tortillas into quarters and then cut them in half, to make 32 triangles. Lay them on baking trays.

2. **Brush** each piece with melted butter and season. Bake for 10–12 minutes or until crisp and golden. Cool completely before eating.

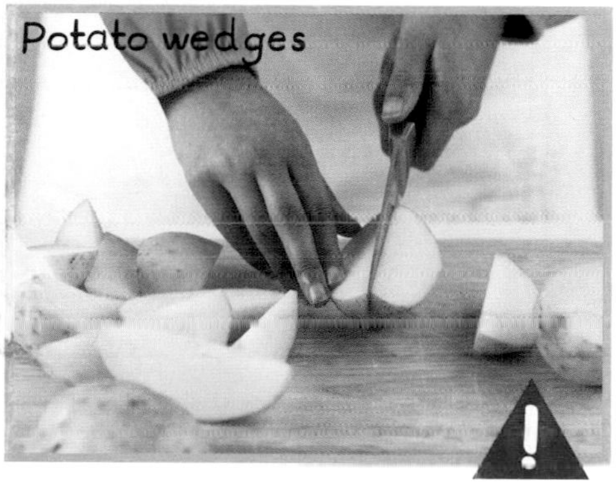

1. Preheat the oven to 425°F. Scrub each potato, pat dry, and cut them in half lengthwise. Cut each half into three equal wedges.

2. Mix the oil, paprika, salt, and pepper in a roasting pan. **Coat** the wedges in the mixture and bake for 40–45 minutes. Shake the pan occasionally.

1. Drain and then rinse the chickpeas. Put them in the food processor, add the remaining hummus ingredients, and **blend** until smooth. Serve.

1. Working around the stone, cut the avocados in half. Scoop out the stone and then the avocado flesh. Finely **chop** the flesh and put it into a bowl.

2. Put the onion, garlic, lime juice, tomato, hot sauce, and cilantro in the mixing bowl. Season and then mix all the ingredients together. Serve.

medium 2 • **preparation** 15-20 minutes • **cooking** 35 minutes

Tomato soup

Soup is the perfect choice for a light meal or as a starter for a special dinner party. This recipe for thick and tasty tomato soup includes carrots, thyme, and garlic for extra flavor and is topped with cubes of toasted bread, called croûtons.

Tools

- ❑ medium saucepan
- ❑ cutting board
- ❑ sharp knife
- ❑ wooden spatula
- ❑ bread knife
- ❑ nonstick baking tray
- ❑ blender
- ❑ ladle
- ❑ peeler
- ❑ oven mitts

Ingredients for 2–4 servings

1 small onion

1 small carrot

2 Tbsp olive oil

1 garlic clove, crushed (optional)

1 Tbsp flour

15-oz can chopped tomatoes

1 Tbsp tomato paste

1 pinch of sugar

black pepper

1 tsp fresh thyme leaves (optional)

2 cups vegetable stock

1 squeeze of fresh lemon juice

For the croûtons

2 thick slices bread

2 Tbsp olive oil

salt and pepper

1. Preheat the oven to 425°F. **Peel** and **chop** the onion and carrot (see p.122). Heat the oil in the saucepan, over medium heat.

2. Add the onion and carrot and cook for about 5 minutes to soften, stirring occasionally. Stir in the garlic and flour and cook the mixture for 1 minute.

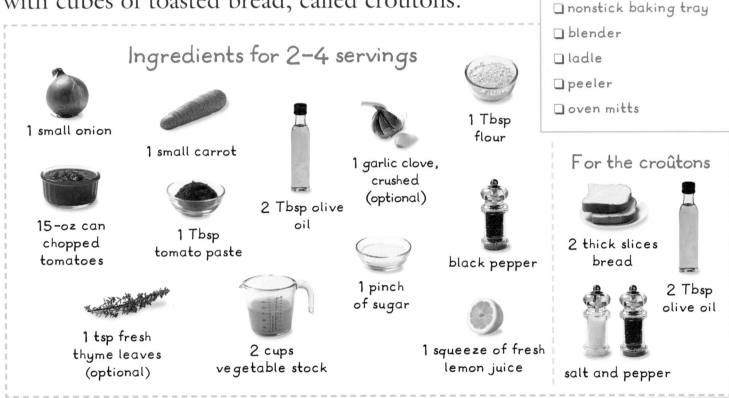

3. Add the tomatoes, paste, thyme, stock, sugar, and lemon juice to the pan and bring to a boil. Reduce the heat and **simmer** for 20–25 minutes.

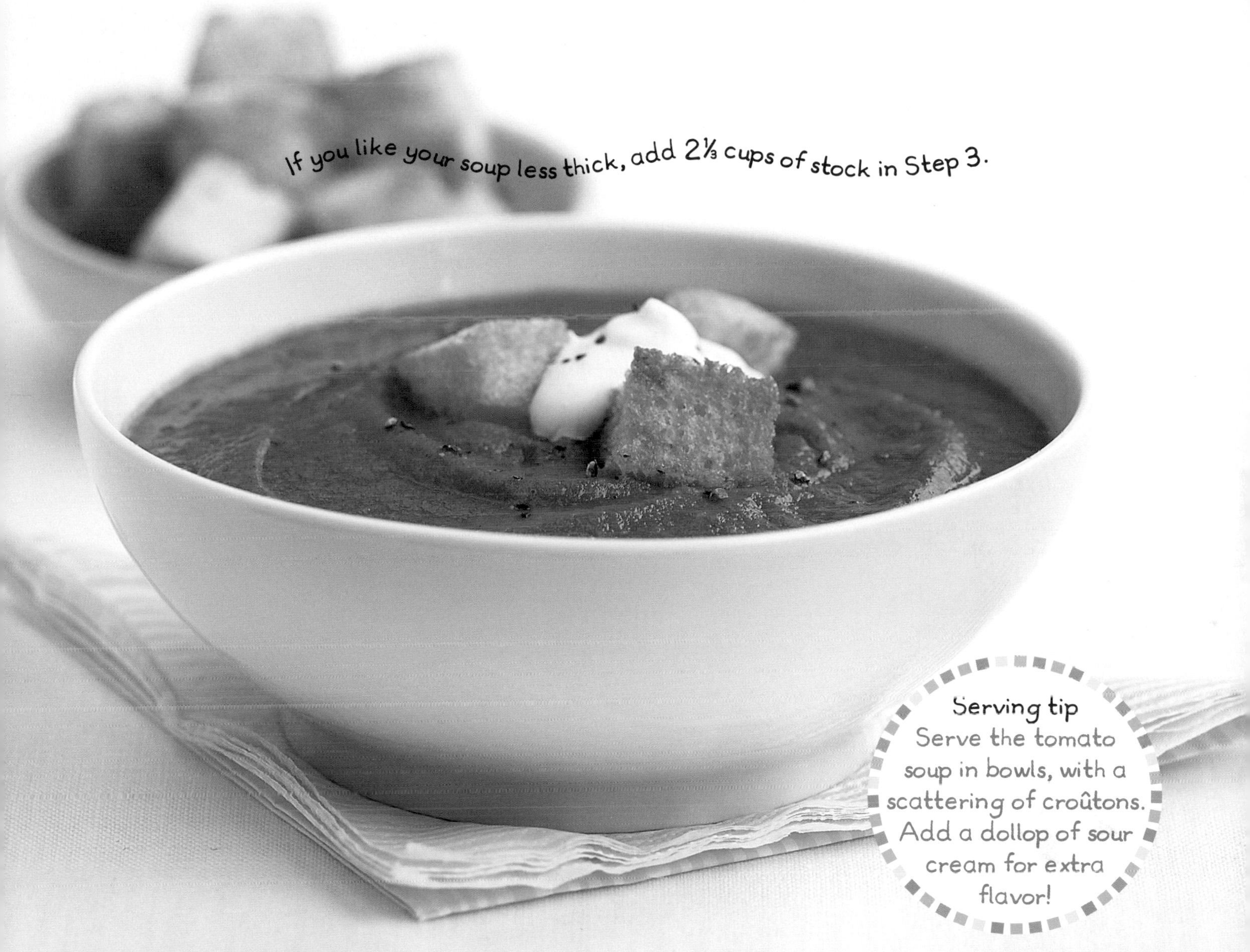

If you like your soup less thick, add 2⅓ cups of stock in Step 3.

Serving tip
Serve the tomato soup in bowls, with a scattering of croûtons. Add a dollop of sour cream for extra flavor!

4. Meanwhile, cut the bread into ¾-inch cubes. Scatter the bread on the baking tray and **drizzle** with the olive oil. Season with salt and pepper.

5. Use your hands to **coat** the the bread in the oil. Bake for 8–10 minutes, until crisp and golden. Shake the tray every few minutes for even cooking.

6. Carefully ladle the hot soup into the blender. Season the soup with pepper, and **blend** until smooth. Ladle the soup into bowls and serve.

medium 2 • **preparation** 20 minutes • **marinating** 30 minutes (optional) • **cooking** 10 minutes

Marinated chicken

The chicken in this recipe is marinated so that it absorbs the curry flavor. If you don't have time, you can leave out the marinating and go straight to cooking in Step 3. Alternatively, you could marinate it longer for a more intense flavor.

Tools

- ❑ mixing bowl
- ❑ dessert spoon
- ❑ 2 cutting boards
- ❑ 2 sharp knives
- ❑ frying pan
- ❑ wooden spatula

Ingredients for 2–4 servings

½ cup plain yogurt

1 Tbsp curry powder

2 Tbsp vegetable oil

juice of ½ lemon

1 tsp tomato paste

2 Tbsp mango chutney (optional)

3 Tbsp raisins (optional)

salt and pepper

2 chicken breasts (skinless and boneless)

3 Tbsp flaked almonds (optional)

To serve

naan bread (see p.106–107)

1–2 small heads of lettuce

Recipe idea
Leave out the almonds and raisins for a plainer dish. Or try serving with a baked potato instead of naan bread (see p.28–29.)

1. In a bowl, **mix** the tomato paste, oil, and curry powder together to make a paste. Add the lemon juice and half the yogurt to make the marinade.

2. On the meat cutting board, carefully cut each chicken breast into **cubes** of about 1 in. (See p.122 for expert tips on slicing, dicing, and cubing.)

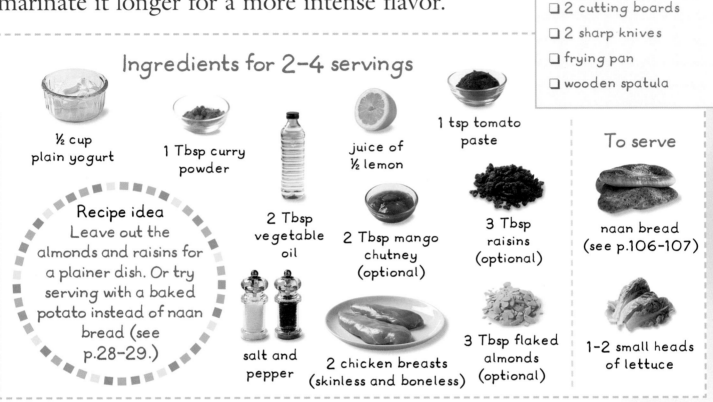

3. Stir the chicken into the marinade, season with salt and pepper, and cover the bowl. Let the chicken **marinate** in the refrigerator for 30 minutes.

See p.123 for tips on how to check whether meat is properly cooked.

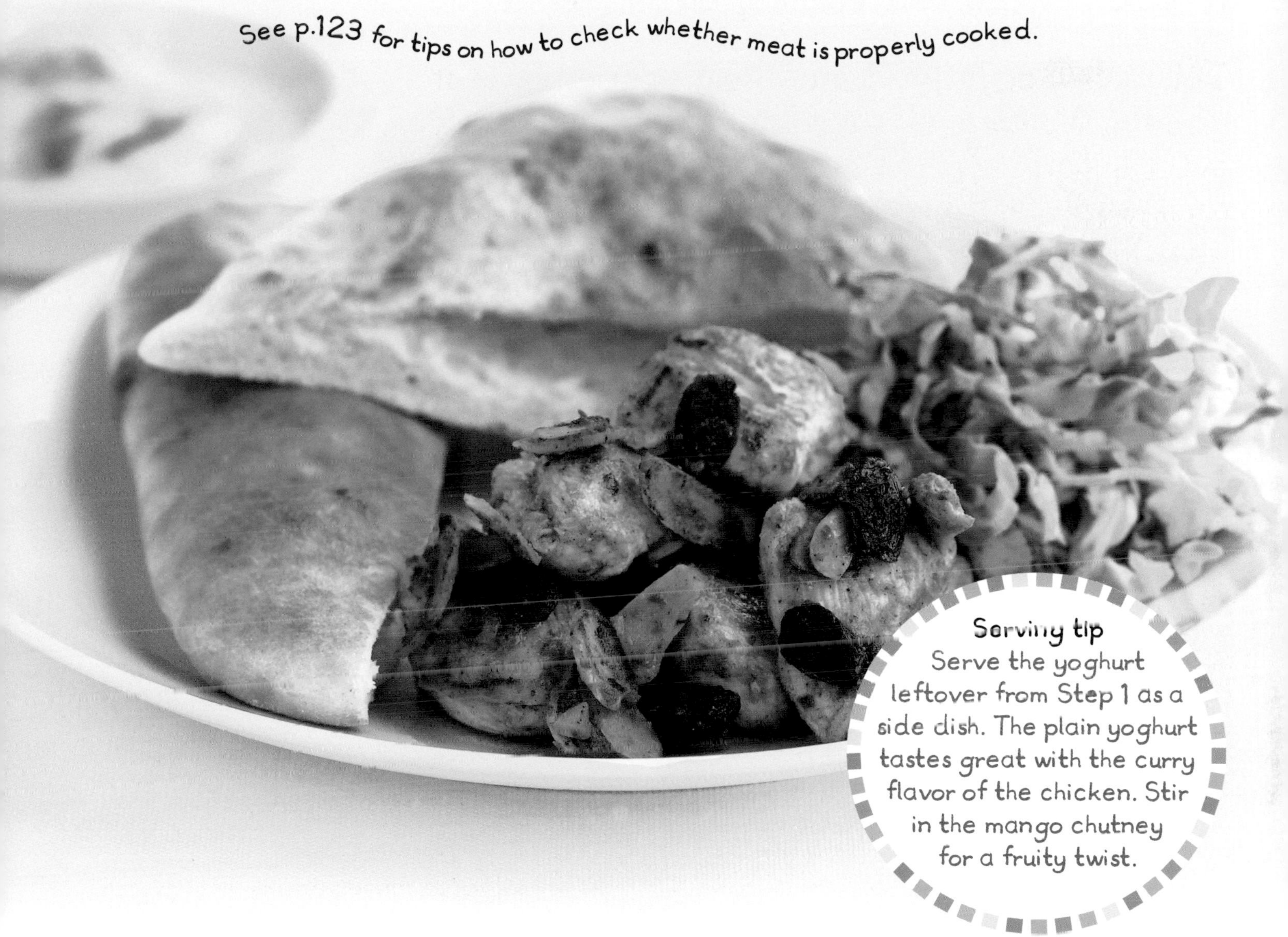

Serving tip
Serve the yoghurt leftover from Step 1 as a side dish. The plain yoghurt tastes great with the curry flavor of the chicken. Stir in the mango chutney for a fruity twist.

4. Place the frying pan over medium to high heat and **fry** the chicken for 3–4 minutes. The chicken will change color, but it will not be cooked yet.

5. Add the raisins and almonds and cook for 3–4 minutes. Before serving, cut a piece of chicken in half. If there is no trace of pink, it is cooked.

6. To shred the lettuce, roll up the leaves and carefully cut them into thin slices. Serve the chicken with the shredded lettuce and naan bread.

medium 2 • **preparation** 20-25 minutes • **cooking** 10-15 minutes

Pesto toast

This recipe introduces you to stove-top grilling, which gives the bread a distinctive pattern. Grilling is also a low-fat way of cooking meat or fish, since the ridged design of the pan helps any excess fat to drain away.

Tools

- ❑ sharp knife
- ❑ cutting board
- ❑ food processor
- ❑ pastry brush
- ❑ grill pan or toaster
- ❑ tongs
- ❑ table knife
- ❑ oven mitts
- ❑ foil-lined broiler pan and rack

Ingredients for 4 servings

For the pesto

1 garlic clove

¼ cup fresh Parmesan cheese

1 Tbsp pine nuts

black pepper

1 cup fresh basil leaves

3 Tbsp olive oil

For the toast

fresh, crusty bread

1 Tbsp olive oil

1 pepper (roasted, skinned, and deseeded)

1 small ball mozzarella (drained)

Recipe idea
The remaining pesto will stay fresh for up to a week if you keep it in an airtight container in the refrigerator. Try stirring it into some pasta for a deliciously simple main meal.

1. Roughly **chop** the garlic and Parmesan cheese and put them in the food processor. Add the pine nuts and make sure the lid is on securely.

2. **Blend** the garlic, Parmesan, and pine nuts until they look like fine breadcrumbs. Add the basil and oil and blend again to make a smooth mixture. Season.

3. Cut 4 slices of bread, about 1 inch thick, and brush both sides with the olive oil. Place the grill pan over medium-high heat.

You can buy roasted peppers in some supermarkets, or roast them yourself (see p.123.)

Chef's tip
For a super-quick snack, skip the broiling part in Step 6. Pesto toast doesn't need to be cooked to taste great!

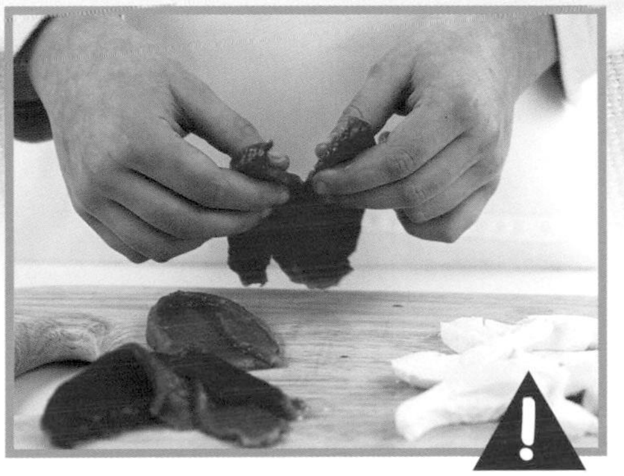

4. **Grill** the bread for 2–3 minutes on each side or until toasted. Don't worry if you don't have a grill pan—broil or toast the bread instead.

5. Slice the ball of mozzarella into 4 equal slices. Tear the pepper and mozzarella into smaller pieces. Preheat the broiler to medium heat.

6. Spread each piece of toast with a layer of pesto and add pepper and mozzarella. **Broil** for 3 minutes or until the cheese melts. Season and serve.

medium 2 • **preparation** 15 minutes • **cooking** 15–20 minutes

Cheese melt with poached egg

Adding a poached egg makes this recipe a tasty variation of toasted cheese. It can be made with any type of bread or cheese.

Ingredients for 2 servings

2 bread rolls, English muffins, or bagels (halved)

2 slices ham (halved)

salt and pepper

a few dashes Worcestershire sauce (optional)

1 egg (beaten)

1 cup cheddar cheese (grated)

2 eggs

Recipe idea
Leave out the egg or ham if you prefer a plain cheese melt.

Tools

- ❑ mixing bowl
- ❑ foil-lined broiler pan and rack
- ❑ 2 teaspoons
- ❑ wooden spoon
- ❑ medium saucepan
- ❑ measuring cup
- ❑ slotted spoon

1. Preheat the broiler to medium heat. **Mix** the grated cheese, Worcestershire sauce, beaten egg, and seasoning together in a small bowl.

2. **Toast** the rolls on both sides, using a broiler or toaster. Place a piece of ham on each half and top with the cheese mix. **Broil** until melted and golden.

3. Crack an egg into a measuring cup and gently tip it into a pan half-full of simmering water. **Simmer** for 3 minutes or until the egg white is cooked.

4. Remove the **poached** egg with a slotted spoon and serve on top of two cheesy melts. Repeat Step 3 with the second egg, season, and serve.

Chef's tip
Line the broiler pan with foil and place the rack on top. This makes the pan easy to wash because any drips or spills will land on the foil, which can be thrown away.

Cheese melts taste great with a green salad (see p. 26–27 for the recipe).

medium 2

• **preparation** 20–25 minutes • **chilling** 30 minutes • **cooking** 15–20 minutes

Hamburgers

This family favorite tastes great when you make it yourself and is lower in fat and higher in taste than store-bought burgers. See p.66–67 for ideas on how to adapt this recipe to make meatballs.

Tools

- ❑ cutting board
- ❑ sharp knife
- ❑ food processor
- ❑ large mixing bowl
- ❑ wooden spoon
- ❑ large plate
- ❑ plastic wrap
- ❑ colander
- ❑ foil-lined broiler pan and rack
- ❑ spatula

Ingredients for 6 burgers

1 lb lean ground beef

½ small red onion (roughly chopped)

2 Tbsp ketchup

1 tsp mustard (optional)

salt and pepper

1 Tbsp Worcestershire sauce (optional)

1 egg yolk (optional)

1 garlic clove (optional)

For the toppings

2 tomatoes

lettuce leaves

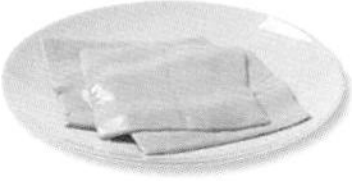

6 cheese slices

6 burger buns

1. Roughly **chop** the onion and garlic. Finely **blend** them and put them in a bowl. Add the beef, Worcestershire sauce, ketchup, mustard, and egg yolk.

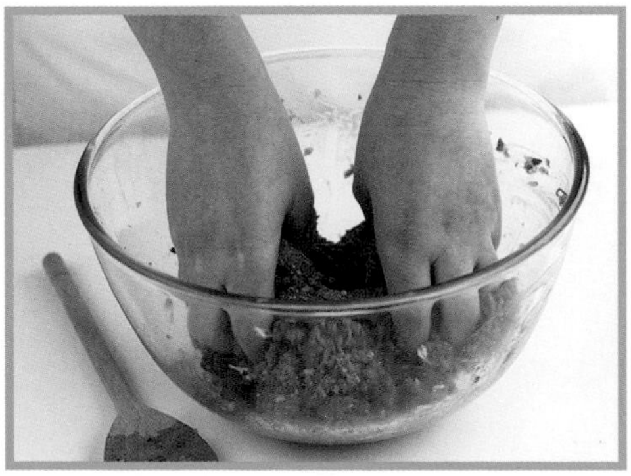

2. Season with salt and pepper and **mix** together. It is easiest to start with a spoon and then use your hands to mix everything together completely.

3. Use your hands to **shape** the mixture into 6 equal-sized balls. Press the top of the balls down to make a flatter burger shape, about ½ inch thick.

In summertime, these burgers taste great cooked on an outdoor grill!

Serving tip
Place the burgers and toppings on a bun, with some ketchup and mayonnaise on the side. Eat with your fingers!

4. Put the burgers on a plate and cover them with plastic wrap. Chill for 30 minutes to make the burgers firmer and easier to cook.

5. Preheat the broiler to medium heat. Place the burgers on a broiler pan and **broil** them for 6–7 minutes on each side or until thoroughly cooked.

6. While the burgers are cooking, prepare the toppings. Wash the lettuce and tomatoes. Halve the burger buns and then thinly slice the tomatoes.

• **preparation** 15 minutes • **cooking** 20 minutes

Pasta salad

Pasta is high in carbohydrates, so it's a great source of energy. This recipe also has eggs and tuna for protein, while the beans and tomatoes provide essential vitamins and minerals. Tuna and other oily fish are very good for you, and you should try to eat them twice a week.

Tools

- ❑ large saucepan
- ❑ slotted spoon
- ❑ colander
- ❑ sieve
- ❑ plate
- ❑ small saucepan
- ❑ bowl of cold water
- ❑ sharp knife
- ❑ cutting board
- ❑ jar with lid
- ❑ metal mixing spoon
- ❑ large mixing bowl

Ingredients for 4–6 servings

½ lb dried penne pasta

1 pinch of salt

1 cup green beans (trimmed and halved)

1 small can tuna

2 green onions (trimmed and sliced)

2 eggs

salt and pepper

4 plum tomatoes (cut into wedges)

16 black olives, halved (optional)

Recipe idea

Other pasta shapes could be used for this recipe. You could also use corn instead of green beans and cooked chicken instead of tuna.

For the dressing

5 Tbsp olive oil

2 Tbsp white wine vinegar

2 tsp whole grain mustard

1. Fill two-thirds of the large saucepan with water and bring it to a boil. Season with a pinch of salt, add the pasta, and **boil** for 12–14 minutes.

2. When the pasta has been cooking for about 6–7 minutes add the green beans to the pan. Finish cooking and drain the pasta and beans in a colander.

3. **Refresh** the pasta and beans with cold water. Drain the tuna in a sieve over a small bowl, and then use your fingers to break it into small flakes.

Pasta cooking times vary, so make sure you check the box.

Chef's tip
Check out p.14–15 for more information on hard-boiling eggs. And see p.125 for more egg tips.

4. Hard-boil the eggs for 6–7 minutes and put them in cold water. Tap the cooled eggs to crack the shell. **Peel** the eggs and cut them into wedges.

5. Spoon the olive oil, white wine vinegar, and mustard into a jar. Screw the lid on tightly and shake the jar vigorously to mix the dressing.

6. Mix the pasta and half of the dressing. **Fold** in the tomatoes, beans, tuna, onions, olives, and remaining dressing. Season and serve with some wedges of egg.

hard 3 • **preparation** 35–45 minutes • **cooking** 20 minutes

Cheese and potato pockets

Puff pastry is really difficult to make at home, so even some of the best chefs buy it ready-made! It is very versatile and can be used for sweet or savory pies and pastries.

Tools

- ❑ small saucepan
- ❑ slotted spoon
- ❑ wooden spoon
- ❑ frying pan or sauté pan
- ❑ saucer or small plate (approx. 5 in in diameter)
- ❑ knife
- ❑ mixing bowl
- ❑ metal mixing spoon
- ❑ fork
- ❑ pastry brush
- ❑ oven mitts
- ❑ large nonstick baking tray

Ingredients for 8 pockets

½ lb potatoes (peeled and diced)

1 pinch of salt

1 Tbsp olive oil

2 x 12-oz ready-rolled puff pastry sheets

1 onion (peeled and diced)

flour (for rolling)

2 cups cheddar cheese (grated)

1 egg (for glazing)

salt and pepper

Recipe idea

Try other fillings, such as spinach, mushrooms, or bacon, but make sure that you cook them as in Steps 1 and 2. You could even try a sweet filling such as the apple pie mixture from p.116–117.

Food fact
Brushing the pockets with beaten egg gives the pastry a golden glaze when it is cooked. You could also use milk for this.

Serving tip
Allow the pockets to cool for at least 5 minutes before you eat them, because they will be really hot!

1. Preheat the oven to 425°F. Half-fill a pan with water and bring to a boil. Add the potatoes and a pinch of salt and bring back to a boil.

2. **Parboil** the potatoes for 5–7 minutes and drain them. Heat the oil and gently **fry** the onion for 2 minutes, to soften. Leave the onion and potatoes to cool.

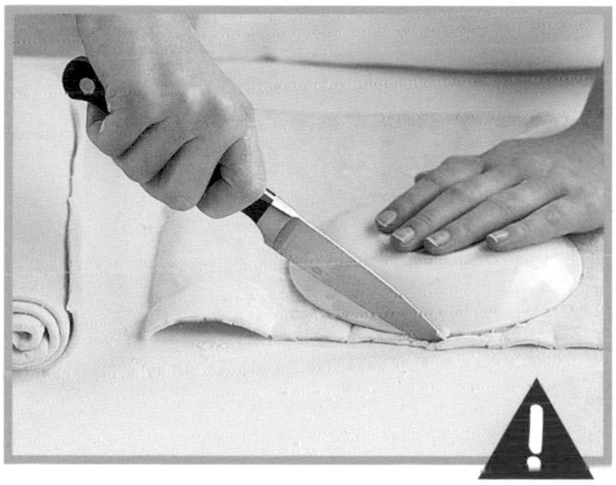

3. Unroll the pastry sheets onto a lightly-floured surface. Using an upside-down saucer or small plate as a template, cut out 8 circles of pastry.

4. Put the cooled potato and onion into a bowl and add the cheese. **Mix** them all together with a metal spoon and season with salt and pepper.

5. Beat the egg lightly with a fork. Brush the edges of each pastry circle with the beaten egg. This will help the pastry stick together.

6. Place some of the cheese and potato mixture in the center of each pastry circle. Bring the edges together to enclose the filling and form a semicircle.

7. Gently **crimp** the edges by pinching the pastry in opposite directions. **Glaze** the pockets with beaten egg and bake for 20 minutes or until golden.

hard 3 • **preparation** 30-35 minutes • **cooking** 5-10 minutes

Falafel with tzatziki

Falafel is a spicy chickpea patty that originally came from the Middle East. Chickpeas are part of a food group called legumes, which are a good source of protein, vitamins, and minerals and are also high in fiber.

Tools

- ❑ food processor
- ❑ medium frying pan
- ❑ slotted metal spatula
- ❑ plate
- ❑ paper towels
- ❑ grater
- ❑ cutting board
- ❑ dish towel
- ❑ small bowl
- ❑ mixing bowl
- ❑ dessert spoon

Ingredients for 12 falafel

15-oz can chickpeas (drained)

2–3 sprigs fresh parsley (torn)

½ small onion (chopped)

1 tsp ground cumin

1 tsp fresh lemon juice

1 tsp ground coriander

1 garlic clove (chopped)

2 Tbsp flour+ extra for shaping

salt and pepper

1 cup sunflower oil

Recipe idea

Try other canned legumes, such as kidney beans, butter beans, cannellini beans, or black-eyed peas.

For the tzatziki

½ cucumber

1 Tbsp chopped fresh mint (optional)

salt and pepper

1 garlic clove (crushed, optional)

1 cup plain yogurt

1. Put the chickpeas, onion, garlic, cumin, coriander, flour, and parsley into the food processor and **blend** them together, until they are smooth.

2. Lightly flour the work surface and turn out the mixture. Divide into 12 equal portions and **shape** each portion into a flat, round patty.

3. Pour the oil into the frying pan and heat it over medium-high heat. **Shallow-fry** the falafel for 2–3 minutes on each side, or until golden and crisp.

Serving tip
The falafel and tzatziki taste great served with, or inside, pita bread!

To deseed a cucumber, slice it in half lengthwise and scoop out the seeds with a teaspoon.

4. Take the cooked falafel out of the frying pan with a slotted metal spatula. Place them on a plate lined with paper towels to drain the excess oil.

5. **Deseed** and then **grate** the cucumber. Wrap the cucumber in a clean dish towel and firmly squeeze out any excess moisture into a small bowl.

6. **Mix** together the grated cucumber, yogurt, lemon juice, mint, and garlic. Season with salt and pepper and serve the tzatziki with the falafel.

• **preparation** 20 minutes • **cooking** 20 minutes

Sushi rolls

Impress your friends with these sophisticated sushi rolls. Once you have mastered the rolling technique in Steps 5–7, they are quite simple. This recipe makes 4 long rolls with a carrot or cucumber filling, which you can then cut up into delicious bite-sized pieces.

Tools

- ❑ medium saucepan with lid
- ❑ serving spoon
- ❑ small saucepan
- ❑ wooden spoon
- ❑ shallow dish (approx. 6 in x 8 in)
- ❑ plastic wrap
- ❑ teaspoon
- ❑ cutting board
- ❑ sharp knife
- ❑ bamboo sushi mat or squares of plastic wrap
- ❑ plate

Ingredients for 4 long rolls

¾ cup sushi rice (rinsed)

1½ cups water

½ tsp table salt

2 Tbsp rice wine vinegar

1 Tbsp sugar

4 seaweed (nori) sheets

For the filling

½ small cucumber (halved lengthwise)

or

½ carrot (peeled and halved lengthwise)

For dipping

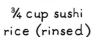

soy sauce

Recipe idea

Experiment with alternative sushi fillings such as tofu, tuna, salmon, crab meat, cheese, avocado, or peppers.

Serving tip

Put the rolls onto a plate, cover with cling film, and chill for at least 1 hour. When the rolls are ready, rinse a sharp knife under cold water and slice them into 5 or 6 pieces.

1. Add the rice and water to the pan and cover with a lid. Bring to a boil and then reduce the heat. **Simmer** for 10 minutes. Remove the pan from the heat.

2. Leave the covered rice to stand for 10 minutes or until the liquid has been absorbed. Meanwhile, **warm** the vinegar, sugar, and salt until dissolved.

3. Line a shallow dish with plastic wrap. Stir the sweetened vinegar mixture into the rice, then carefully pack it into the dish. Leave to cool.

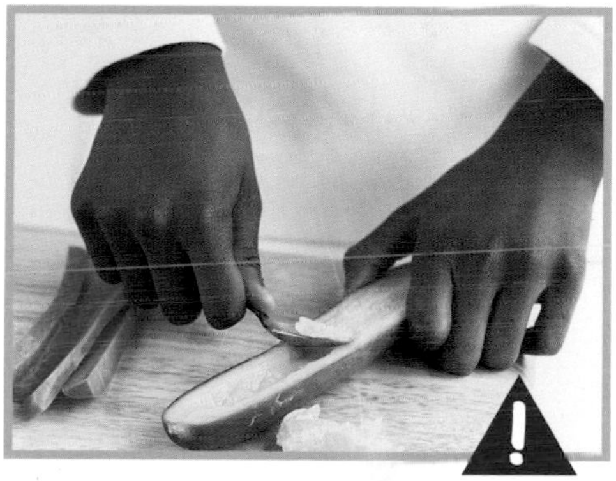

4. **Deseed** the cucumber, using a teaspoon and then **slice** it into four equal strips. If you are using carrot instead, cut it into 4 long strips.

5. Place a seaweed sheet, shiny side down, on a bamboo mat. Dip your hands in water and pat a quarter of the rice onto two-thirds of the sheet.

6. Lay a piece of cucumber or carrot widthways along the center of the rice. Holding the mat, **roll** the nori over and over, to the edge of the rice.

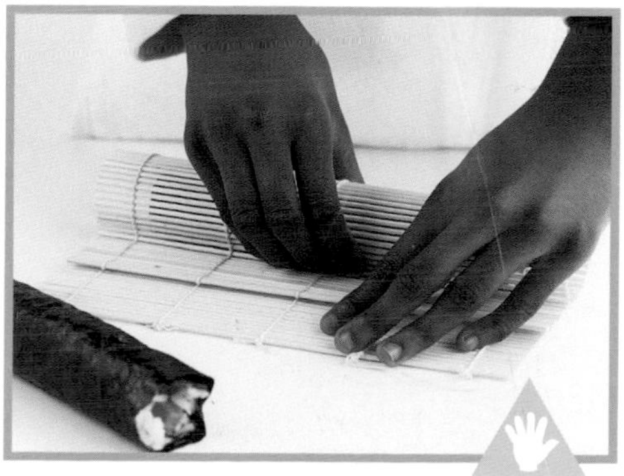

7. Tuck the rolled edge of the nori firmly under the filling. Dampen the remaining nori and roll to seal. Using the mat, pull the roll tightly to seal.

Main meals

It's vital to have one substantial main meal every day. Most people eat their main meal at the end of the day, when they have more time to prepare and enjoy it. If you have your main meal in the evening, it is important not to eat just before you go to bed, or your food will not be properly digested and a full stomach might keep you awake!

There's nothing more satisfying than eating something that you've prepared yourself! In this section, you'll find some of your favorite recipes, but you will also be able to experiment with new ingredients and types of food as well as learning some new cooking skills.

Noodle soup

This is a healthy, filling, and complete meal in a bowl. Best of all, it only uses one pan, so there's less to wash afterward!

Ingredients for 2 servings

2 tsp vegetable oil

2 green onions (trimmed and sliced diagonally)

1 thin slice fresh ginger, peeled (optional)

juice of ½ lime

2 ½ cups fish stock

2 ½ oz fine egg noodles

1 tsp soy sauce

½ cup baby corn (halved)

½ cup sugar snap peas

1 drop of sesame oil

¼ lb ready-to-cook raw shrimp (shelled)

2 tsp fresh cilantro, chopped (optional)

Tools

- ❑ medium saucepan
- ❑ wooden spoon
- ❑ measuring cup

1. Heat the vegetable oil in a medium saucepan. Gently **fry** the spring onions over medium heat for 1–2 minutes, until soft.

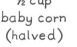

2. Stir the ginger, stock, lime juice, and soy sauce into the spring onions and bring to the boil. Lower the heat and then **simmer** for 2–3 minutes.

3. Remove the ginger. Add the noodles and corn and bring to a boil. After 1½ minutes, add the sugar snap peas and cook for 1½ minutes more.

4. Lower the heat to bring the soup back to a simmer. Stir in the shrimp and cook them for 2–3 minutes, or until pink. Stir in the sesame oil and cilantro.

Raw shrimp are gray or white in color, but they turn pink when they are cooked!

Food fact

Don't overcook the shrimp or they will get rubbery! And if you use frozen shrimp, make sure you defrost them completely before cooking them.

Chicken wraps

The combination of red and yellow peppers and green snow peas makes these wraps look really colorful, and the simple flavoring gives the chicken a refreshing, zingy taste. See p.123 for tips on how to check whether your chicken is cooked properly.

Don't overcook the vegetables—they taste better slightly crunchy!

Tools

- ❑ 2 cutting boards
- ❑ 1 sharp knife
- ❑ vegetable knife
- ❑ medium bowl
- ❑ small whisk
- ❑ large frying pan
- ❑ wooden spatula
- ❑ ovenproof plate
- ❑ kitchen foil
- ❑ oven mitts
- ❑ tongs

Ingredients for 8 wraps

4 skinless and boneless chicken breasts (cut into 24 strips)

1 small yellow pepper

1 small red pepper

1 cup snow peas

8 flour tortillas

juice of ½ lime

For the flavoring

1 inch fresh ginger, peeled and grated (optional)

2 Tbsp honey

1 pinch of salt

1 Tbsp sunflower oil

3–4 dashes of hot sauce (optional)

Recipe idea
Vegetarians could use tofu instead of chicken, or double the amount of vegetables.

Serving tip
Chicken wraps taste great served with guacamole (see p. 30–31 for the recipe) and sour cream on the side.

1. Preheat the oven to 400°F. **Deseed** both peppers and slice them into 12 equal strips. (See p.122 for expert tips on how to do this.)

2. **Mix** together the oil, honey, ginger, hot sauce, and salt. Stir in the chicken strips until they are all completely coated with the flavoring.

Chef's tip
In Step 5 the chicken and vegetables will continue to cook in the hot frying pan, so serve immediately or transfer them to a serving dish.

3. Heat the frying pan for 2 minutes. Add the coated chicken and **fry** it for 4–5 minutes. The chicken will turn golden and then caramelize.

4. Place the tortillas on the ovenproof plate and cover with foil. Put them in the preheated oven for 6–7 minutes, or until they are warmed through.

5. Add the peppers, snow peas, and lime juice to the chicken. Cook for 4–5 minutes on medium-high heat. Stir occasionally to prevent sticking.

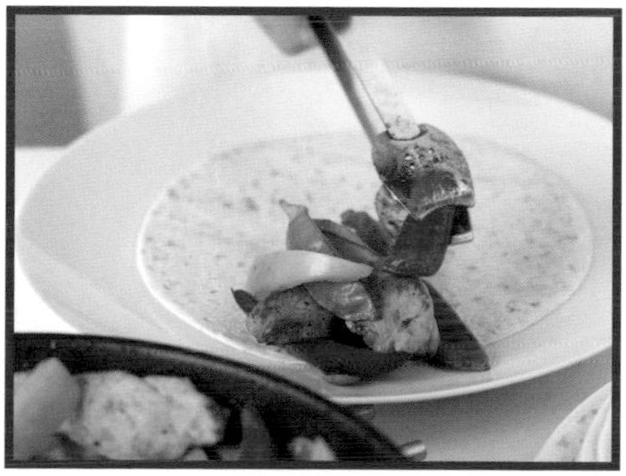

6. Lay some of the filling along the top of each tortilla, leaving the other end and sides empty. If you overfill your tortilla, you will not be able to wrap it.

7. To wrap, fold the empty end inward and overlap the sides. The filling should be securely wrapped but will peep out appetizingly from the open end!

• **preparation** 20 minutes • **cooking** 35–40 minutes

Pepperoni pasta

This delicious recipe provides a wide range of nutrients, from carbohydrates in the pasta to protein in the sausage, and vitamins in the tomatoes and peppers.

Tools

- ❑ 2 cutting boards
- ❑ sharp knife
- ❑ garlic press
- ❑ 2 large saucepans
- ❑ wooden spoon
- ❑ slotted metal spoon
- ❑ colander
- ❑ pasta spoon

Ingredients for 4–6 servings

2 garlic cloves

1 red onion

1 tsp dried oregano

2 red peppers (roasted, peeled, and deseeded)

4 oz pepperoni

1 cup vegetable stock

4 dashes of hot sauce (optional)

2 Tbsp sun-dried tomato paste

15-oz can chopped tomatoes

1 Tbsp olive oil

1 tsp Worcestershire sauce (optional)

1 Tbsp sugar

salt and pepper

2 oz per person, spaghetti

10 fresh basil leaves (torn)

Recipe idea
Any type of cooked or cured sausage would taste delicious in this recipe, and if you don't have sun-dried tomato paste, use regular tomato paste.

1. **Dice** the red onion and roasted peppers. Peel and **crush** the garlic cloves.(See p.122 for expert dicing and crushing tips.)

2. Carefully cut the pepperoni into diagonal slices, about ¾ in thick. Add the oil to a saucepan and heat it gently, over a medium heat.

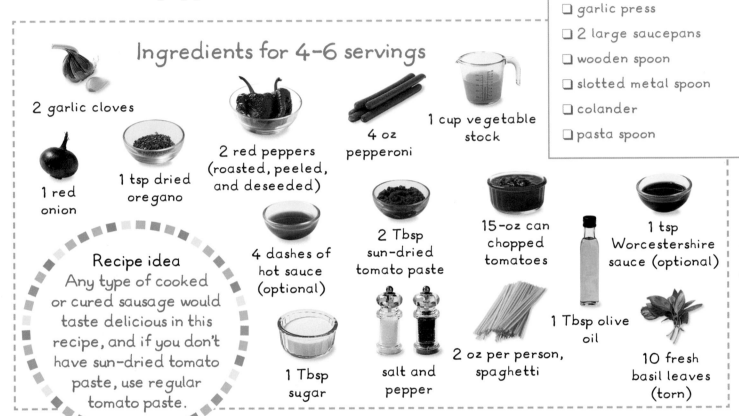

3. **Sauté** the onion for 2–3 minutes. Add the garlic and oregano and cook for 1–2 minutes. Add the pepperoni and cook for 2 minutes more.

A sprinkling of freshly grated Parmesan cheese tastes great!

Serving tip
Use the pasta spoon to transfer the spaghetti into pasta bowls. Serve the sauce on top of the spaghetti.

4. Add the tomatoes, tomato paste, peppers, sugar, stock, Worcestershire sauce, and hot sauce. Bring to a boil, season, and **simmer** for 20 minutes.

5. Half-fill a large saucepan with water and bring it to a boil. Add a pinch of salt, then lower the spaghetti into the pan with a slotted spoon.

6. Boil the pasta for 10–12 minutes (check the exact timing on the package). Drain the pasta and then stir the fresh basil into the tomato sauce.

medium 2 • **preparation** 15 minutes • **marinating** 1 hour • **cooking** 25–30 minutes

Barbecue chicken

Marinating is a simple but effective way of adding extra flavor to meat, fish, and vegetables. Soaking these chicken pieces in a marinade for at least an hour before you cook them gives them a delicious barbecue taste. On a warm summer day, they could be cooked on an outdoor grill.

Tools

- ❑ whisk
- ❑ small mixing bowl
- ❑ large dish (approx. 2 in deep)
- ❑ paper towels
- ❑ sharp knife
- ❑ cutting board
- ❑ oven mitts
- ❑ plastic wrap
- ❑ foil-lined broiler pan
- ❑ kitchen tongs
- ❑ dessert spoon

Ingredients for 4 servings

8 chicken drumsticks

2 Tbsp ketchup

2 Tbsp soy sauce

3 Tbsp honey

2 Tbsp fresh orange juice

1 Tbsp sunflower oil

1 garlic clove (crushed)

1 tsp mustard

Recipe idea
Chicken breasts or thighs also taste great cooked this way, but always make sure the meat is completely cooked. (See p.123 for tips on this.)

1. Put all the ingredients except the chicken drumsticks in a bowl and **whisk** them together. Pour the mixture into a large, shallow dish.

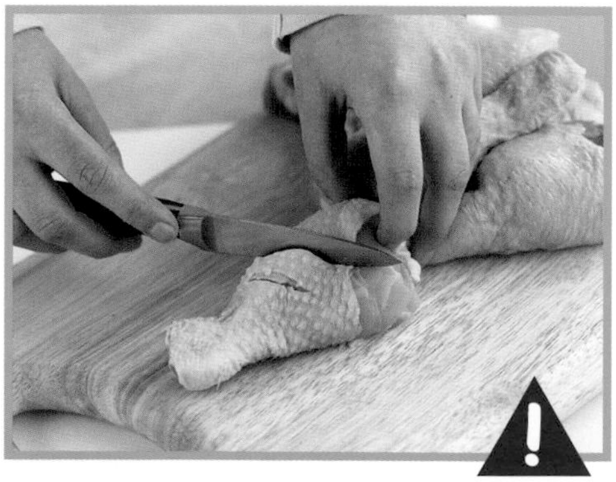

2. Pat the chicken pieces with paper towels. Make 3 deep cuts in each drumstick. This is known as **scoring** and helps the meat to soak up the marinade.

3. Put the chicken in the dish and roll each piece until it is coated with sauce. Cover with plastic wrap and leave to **marinate** in the refrigerator for 1 hour.

Wrap the cooled chicken in a napkin and eat with your fingers!

Safety tip
You must always wash your hands thoroughly after touching raw meat to avoid spreading any germs.

Serving tip
The chicken will need to stand for 2–3 minutes before it is ready to serve.

4. Preheat the broiler to medium heat. Lay the coated chicken (uncut side up) on a foil-lined broiler pan. Put the marinade to one side.

5. **Broil** the chicken pieces for 7–8 minutes. Using tongs, carefully turn the chicken over and broil the other side for 7–8 minutes more.

6. Turn the chicken again. Spoon on half the sauce. Broil for 5 minutes, turn, and spoon on the rest of the sauce. Broil for a final 5 minutes.

Chicken curry

Curry originally came from Asia, and this recipe is influenced by the fragrant curries of Thailand. For an Indian-style curry, skip Step 1 and use double the amount of the paste from p.34–35.

Tools

- ❑ cutting board
- ❑ sharp knife
- ❑ food processor
- ❑ wok or large saucepan
- ❑ wooden spoon
- ❑ medium saucepan with lid
- ❑ measuring cup

Ingredients for 2-4 servings

6 green onions (trimmed and roughly chopped)

For the paste

1 garlic clove

2-in piece fresh ginger (peeled and chopped)

11/4 cups fresh cilantro

1 tsp cilantro seeds, crushed (optional)

2 tsp lemon zest

2 Tbsp olive oil

1 tsp lime zest

1 Tbsp soft dark brown sugar

2-3 drops hot sauce

For the curry

1 cup coconut milk

2 skinless chicken breasts (cubed)

⅓ cup per person long-grain rice

1 cup chicken stock

2 cups button mushrooms (sliced)

3 cups broccoli (cut into florets)

1. **Peel** and **chop** the ginger. Roughly chop the garlic and cilantro. Put all the paste ingredients into a processor and **blend** until smooth.

2. Place a wok or large saucepan over medium heat. Pour in half of the coconut milk and stir in half of the paste. Cook for 1 minute, stirring constantly.

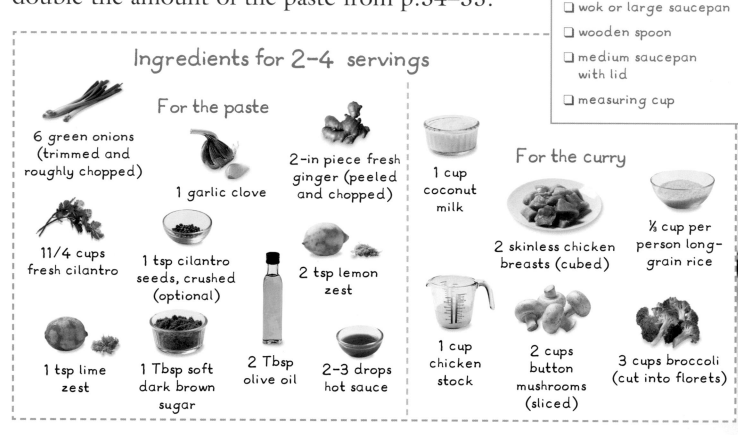

3. Add the chicken and cook it for 3–4 minutes. Rinse the rice with cold water and tip it into a medium saucepan. Add double the amount of water to the rice.

For extra zing, you could add green or red chili peppers instead of the hot sauce in Step 1.

Safety tip
Although the chicken will change color, it will not be completely cooked in Step 3.

4. Allow the rice to boil, cover, and **simmer** until all the water is absorbed. If the rice is not cooked, add more water and cook for a few more minutes.

5. While the rice is cooking, add the remaining coconut milk and paste to the wok. Pour in the stock, stir, and boil for 1 minute. Reduce the heat to a simmer.

6. Add the mushrooms and simmer for 1 minute. Then add the broccoli and simmer for 4–5 minutes more. Serve with the cooked rice.

medium 2

• **preparation** 20 minutes • **cooking** 15–20 minutes

Stir-fry with noodles

Stir-frying is a quick way to cook—the ingredients are stirred continually over a high heat for a short amount of time, so the vegetables remain crunchy. This recipe is made with tofu, a great alternative to meat that is high in protein and calcium.

Tools

- ❑ medium saucepan with lid
- ❑ paper towels
- ❑ cutting board
- ❑ sharp knife
- ❑ measuring cup
- ❑ whisk
- ❑ wok or large frying pan
- ❑ wooden spatula
- ❑ tongs
- ❑ plate
- ❑ colander
- ❑ pasta spoon

Ingredients for 2–4 servings

8 oz firm tofu

2 green onions (trimmed)

1 carrot (peeled)

1 red pepper (deseeded)

2 tsp sunflower oil

½ cup baby corn

2 oz per person, dried medium egg noodles

½ cup unsalted cashews (optional)

½ cup sugar snap peas

For the stir-fry sauce

1 tsp honey

1 Tbsp fresh orange juice

1 tsp sesame oil

1 Tbsp soy sauce

2 Tbsp sunflower oil

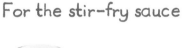

Recipe idea
Chicken or shrimp could be used instead of tofu, but make sure you cook them thoroughly in Step 4.

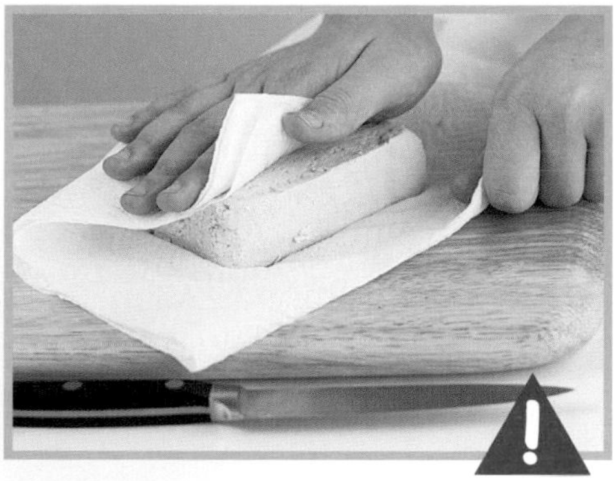

1. Half-fill a medium saucepan with water, cover, and bring to a boil. Drain the tofu and pat it dry with paper towels. Cut the tofu into cubes.

2. Diagonally **slice** the green onions. Cut the carrot in half and then into long sticks. Slice the pepper into strips and cut the corn in half.

Food fact
Cooking vegetables for only a short time means that they retain most of their nutrients, which can sometimes be lost through over-cooking.

3. To make the stir-fry sauce, **whisk** the honey, orange juice, sesame oil, sunflower oil, and soy sauce in a measuring cup until they are fully mixed.

4. Heat half the oil in the wok, and fry the tofu for 7–8 mins, or until it turns golden. Take it out of the wok and place it on a plate lined with paper towels.

5. Lower the noodles into the boiling water. Bring the pan back to a boil and cook the noodles for 4 minutes or as instructed on the package.

6. Use the remaining oil to **stir-fry** the green onions, carrot, and pepper for 2–3 minutes. Add the corn, cashews, peas, and sauce. Stir-fry for 2 minutes.

7. Add the cooked tofu and stir-fry for a further 2 minutes. Drain the noodles and serve the stir-fried vegetables and tofu over the noodles.

medium 2 • **preparation** 25–30 minutes • **cooking** 1 hour

Mashed-potato pies

This recipe is a tasty variation on a traditional shepherd's pie. It is a filling and nutritious main meal and can easily be made with ground beef, pork, lamb, or soy "hamburger." If you don't have four small dishes, you can use one large dish instead.

Always use oven mitts to handle the hot dishes.

Tools

- ❑ cutting board
- ❑ peeler
- ❑ sharp knife
- ❑ garlic press
- ❑ 2 large saucepans
- ❑ wooden spoon
- ❑ colander
- ❑ masher
- ❑ 4 ovenproof dishes
- ❑ large baking tray
- ❑ slotted spoon
- ❑ teaspoon
- ❑ dessert spoon
- ❑ oven mitts

Ingredients for 4 pies

1 Tbsp olive oil

1 carrot

1 onion

2 tsp chopped rosemary leaves (optional)

1 lb lean ground beef

1 garlic clove

1½ cups mushrooms (quartered)

⅔ cup beef stock

1 Tbsp tomato paste

2 tsp Worcestershire sauce (optional)

salt and pepper

15-oz can chopped tomatoes

For the topping

1 lb 2 oz potatoes

1 pinch of salt

2 tbsp milk

2 Tbsp unsalted butter

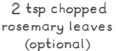

½ cup cheese (grated)

Recipe idea
Try these pies with vegetarian "hamburger" and vegetable stock for a meat-free alternative.

Serving tip
Allow the pies to cool for a few minutes before eating them. They taste great served with vegetables, such as broccoli or peas.

1. Preheat the oven to 400°F. **Peel** and **dice** the onion and carrot. **Crush** the garlic. (See p.122 for expert cutting and crushing tips.)

2. Heat the oil and **fry** the beef for 4 minutes or until browned, stirring constantly. Add the onion, carrot, rosemary, and garlic and fry for 3–5 minutes.

3. Add the mushrooms, stock, tomato paste, Worcestershire sauce, and tomatoes. Bring to a boil and then reduce to a **simmer** for 20 minutes. Season.

4. Half-fill a pan with water and bring it to a boil. Peel and chop the potatoes and add them to the pan, with the salt. Boil for 12–15 minutes, or until soft.

5. Drain the potatoes in a colander and then put them back in the saucepan. **Mash** the potatoes with the milk, butter, and half of the cheese.

6. Place the dishes on a baking tray and divide the meat filling between them, using a slotted spoon. Top each with a quarter of the mashed potatoes.

7. Sprinkle the remaining cheese on top of the mashed potato and bake the pies for 25–30 minutes or until they are golden and bubbling.

hard 3 • **preparation** 35–40 minutes • **chilling** 30 minutes • **cooking** 14–16 minutes

Meatballs with salsa

Give classic meatballs a sweet-and-sour twist with this tasty recipe. Broiling is much healthier than frying, and using skewers (see Steps 4 and 6) makes it much safer and easier to cook the meatballs evenly. When using skewers, you must soak them in water for at least 1 hour so that they don't splinter or burn during cooking.

Chilling the meatballs before cooking stops them from falling apart.

Tools

- ❑ bread knife
- ❑ cutting board
- ❑ food processor
- ❑ 2 large mixing bowls
- ❑ wooden spoon
- ❑ plate
- ❑ plastic wrap
- ❑ dessert spoon
- ❑ 6 wooden skewers
- ❑ oven mitts
- ❑ broiler pan and foil-lined tray
- ❑ fork
- ❑ bowl

Ingredients for 18 meatballs

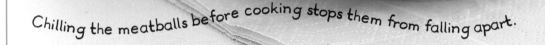

2 medium slices of bread

1 Tbsp soy sauce

½ red onion (roughly chopped)

1 garlic clove (chopped)

1 egg yolk

zest of 1 lime

1 Tbsp ketchup

1 lb ground pork

For the salsa

1 tsp fresh lime juice

1–2 drops of hot sauce (optional)

2–3 pinches of sugar

1 small can pineapple pieces (drained)

12 cherry tomatoes (quartered)

3 green onions (trimmed and finely chopped)

salt and pepper

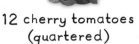

1 tsp olive oil

1. Cut the crusts off and tear the bread into chunks. Put the bread into the food processor and **blend** it until it becomes fine breadcrumbs.

2. Put the breadcrumbs in a bowl. Put the onion and garlic into the food processor and finely blend them. Add them to the bowl of breadcrumbs.

Recipe idea

Use the mixture from the burgers on p.40–41, follow Steps 1–4 on this recipe, and fry the meatballs until cooked through. Serve with tomato sauce (without the pepperoni!) and spaghetti (p.56–57).

3. Add the meat, lime zest, ketchup, soy sauce, and egg yolk to the bowl. Using a wooden spoon or your fingers, **mix** until fully combined.

4. Using your hands, **shape** the meat mixture into 18 equal balls. Place the meatballs on a plate, cover with plastic wrap, and chill for 30 minutes.

5. Put the pineapple into a mixing bowl and stir in the green onions, tomatoes, lime juice, hot sauce, sugar, and olive oil. Season and set aside.

6. Preheat the broiler to medium heat. Carefully place 3 meatballs on each skewer. **Broil** for 14–16 minutes, turning every 3–4 minutes.

7. When the meatballs are cooked completely, use a fork to slide them carefully off the skewers. Serve the meatballs with some salsa on the side.

hard 3 • preparation 35–40 minutes • marinating 1–2 hours • cooking 12–16 minutes

Lamb kebabs

This marinade adds a gentle, spicy flavor to the lamb, while the couscous is very simple to cook and is a great alternative to rice.

Tools

- ❑ 2 mixing bowls
- ❑ dessert spoon
- ❑ plastic wrap
- ❑ cutting board
- ❑ sharp knife
- ❑ 8 wooden skewers
- ❑ broiler pan and foil-lined tray
- ❑ tongs
- ❑ fork
- ❑ oven mitts

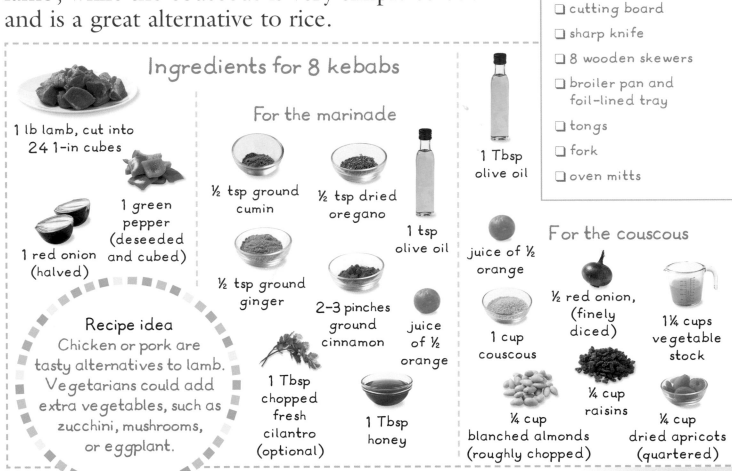

Ingredients for 8 kebabs

1 lb lamb, cut into 24 1-in cubes

1 green pepper (deseeded and cubed)

1 red onion (halved)

For the marinade

½ tsp ground cumin

½ tsp dried oregano

1 tsp olive oil

½ tsp ground ginger

2–3 pinches ground cinnamon

juice of ½ orange

1 Tbsp chopped fresh cilantro (optional)

1 Tbsp honey

1 Tbsp olive oil

juice of ½ orange

For the couscous

1 cup couscous

½ red onion, (finely diced)

1¼ cups vegetable stock

¼ cup blanched almonds (roughly chopped)

¼ cup raisins

¼ cup dried apricots (quartered)

Recipe idea

Chicken or pork are tasty alternatives to lamb. Vegetarians could add extra vegetables, such as zucchini, mushrooms, or eggplant.

1. **Mix** the marinade ingredients together in a bowl. Stir in the lamb and cover with plastic wrap. Leave to **marinate** for 1–2 hours in the refrigerator.

2. Cut each onion half into 4 equal wedges and remove the white core from each piece. Split the wedges in half to make 16 thin pieces of onion.

3. Place a cube of lamb onto a skewer, followed by pieces of onion and pepper. Repeat and add a piece of lamb to finish. Do the same for all 8 skewers.

Chef's tip
Soak the wooden skewers for at least 1 hour before you use them so that they don't burn or splinter in Step 4.

Serving tip
Serve the kebabs on a bed of couscous. Couscous also tastes great plain, so you could skip the second part of Step 6.

4. Preheat the broiler to medium heat. **Broil** the kebabs for 12–16 minutes, turning every 2–3 minutes. Allow to rest before serving.

5. Meanwhile, pour the hot stock over the couscous and mix them together. Cover the bowl with plastic wrap until all the liquid has been absorbed.

6. Fluff the cooked couscous with a fork to separate the grains. Stir in the orange juice, onion, apricots, almonds, raisins, and olive oil.

hard 3 • **preparation** 45–50 minutes • **cooking** 1 hour 15 minutes

Roasted vegetable lasagna

For this recipe, it is important to use the type of dried lasagna that does not need precooking. Check the package to make you sure you buy the right kind. Fresh lasagna would also be fine, but you would have to reduce the cooking time.

Tools

- ❏ cutting board
- ❏ sharp knife
- ❏ roasting pan
- ❏ wooden spoon
- ❏ large saucepan
- ❏ small saucepan
- ❏ whisk
- ❏ measuring cup
- ❏ lasagna dish (approx. 10 x 7 in and 3 in deep)
- ❏ oven mitts
- ❏ serving spoon

Recipe idea

For an alternative filling, try the meat mixture from the Mashed-potato pies on p. 64–65.

Ingredients for 6–8 servings

2 red onions

2 large carrots (peeled)

2 large zucchini

2 red peppers (deseeded)

2 yellow peppers (deseeded)

1 medium eggplant

2 tsp fresh rosemary (chopped)

1 Tbsp tomato paste

4 Tbsp olive oil

2 garlic cloves (crushed)

13-oz can chopped tomatoes

9 dried lasagna sheets

salt and pepper

For the sauce

2 cups warm milk

¼ cup unsalted butter

½ cup flour

salt and pepper

1 cup Parmesan cheese (grated)

1. Preheat the oven to 425°F. Cut the onions into wedges and then **chop** the carrots, zucchini, eggplant, and peppers into chunks.

2. In the roasting pan, mix the oil, rosemary, and garlic with the vegetables and season. **Roast** for 35 minutes, shaking the tin occasionally.

3. Gently **warm** the tomatoes and tomato paste in a large saucepan. Take the pan off the heat and carefully stir in the roasted vegetables.

4. Over low heat, melt the butter in a saucepan. Stir in the flour for 1 minute and **whisk** in the milk. Stir until thickened. Add half the cheese and season.

Chef's tip
If your sauce gets lumpy in Step 4, don't worry! Strain it to remove the lumps before adding the cheese.

5. Reduce the oven to 375°F. Spoon a third of the vegetables into the base of the lasagna dish and top with 3 lasagna sheets.

6. Add another third of the vegetables and pour on half the sauce. Top with another layer of lasagna sheets and add the remaining vegetables.

7. Finally, add the 3 remaining lasagna sheets and sauce. Sprinkle the cheese over the top and bake for 35 minutes or until golden and bubbling.

• **preparation** 30–40 minutes • **chilling** 30 minutes • **cooking** up to 40 minutes

Tuna fishcakes

Like all oily fish, tuna contains vitamins and minerals that are good for the brain, skin, and eyes. This recipe involves shallow frying, like the falafel on p.46–47. This gives the fishcakes a crisp golden coating, but it is important to drain them on paper towels in Step 6 to remove the excess oil.

Tools

- ❑ medium saucepan
- ❑ colander
- ❑ masher
- ❑ mixing bowl
- ❑ fork
- ❑ large plate
- ❑ plastic wrap
- ❑ dish
- ❑ 2 medium plates
- ❑ large frying pan
- ❑ slotted metal spatula
- ❑ paper towels

Ingredients for 8 fishcakes

½ lb potatoes (peeled and chopped)

1 pinch of salt

12 oz canned tuna (drained weight)

2 tsp Dijon mustard

1 green onion (finely chopped)

salt and pepper

2 tsp chopped fresh parsley

¾ cup flour

5 cups breadcrumbs (approx. 7 slices, without crusts)

2 eggs

1 cup vegetable oil

To serve

lettuce leaves

lemon or lime wedges

1. Half-fill the saucepan with water. Add the potatoes and a pinch of salt. Bring the water to a boil and cook for 12–15 minutes or until soft.

2. Thoroughly drain the potatoes and put them back into the pan. **Mash** the potatoes and leave them to one side until they are cool enough to handle in step 4.

3. Break the tuna into small pieces in a bowl. Stir in the mashed potatoes, mustard, green onion, and parsley until they are fully mixed in. Season.

Use tuna packed in water or brine rather than oil, since it is lower in fat.

Chef's tip
Fry the fishcakes in batches of 2 or 4 and keep the cooked ones warm in the oven. Serve with salad and lemon or lime wedges.

4. Lightly dust your hands with flour and **shape** the mixture into 8 cakes. Place the fishcakes on a plate, cover with plastic wrap, and chill for 30 minutes.

5. **Beat** the eggs together in a dish and put the breadcrumbs and flour on separate plates. **Coat** each fishcake in flour, egg, and then breadcrumbs.

6. Heat the oil, over medium heat. **Shallow-fry** the cakes for 2 minutes on each side, or until golden. Drain them on a plate lined with paper towels.

Sausage popovers

The secret to good popovers is to make sure that the oil is very hot in Step 3 before you add the sausages and then the batter in Step 4. Leaving the batter to stand for half an hour before cooking also helps because it gives them a lighter texture.

Tools

- ❑ sieve
- ❑ mixing bowl
- ❑ ramekin
- ❑ whisk
- ❑ oven mitts
- ❑ nonstick 12-cup muffin tray
- ❑ tongs
- ❑ ladle
- ❑ small saucepan
- ❑ wooden spoon
- ❑ small plate

Ingredients for 12 popovers

1 pinch of salt

3 eggs

4 Tbsp vegetable oil

1 cup milk

1 tsp snipped fresh chives (optional)

1¼ cups flour

1 Tbsp wholegrain mustard (optional)

4 long sausages (each cut into 3 pieces)

For the onion gravy

1 Tbsp vegetable oil

1 tsp dark brown soft sugar

1 tsp balsamic vinegar (optional)

1 small red onion (thinly sliced)

1 Tbsp unsalted butter

1¼ cups beef stock

1 Tbsp flour

Chef's tip
For plain popovers, leave out the chives, mustard, and sausage. Heat the oil in the tray, as in Step 3, and cook the batter for 18–20 minutes.

Serving tip
Serve popovers with gravy and vegetables, such as peas. Strain the gravy if you prefer a smoother sauce.

1. Preheat the oven to 425°F. **Sift** the flour and salt into a bowl and make a hole in the center. **Crack** the eggs and add them to the bowl one by one.

2. Using a whisk, **beat** the milk into the eggs and flour until you have a smooth batter, with no lumps. Stir in the chives and mustard (optional).

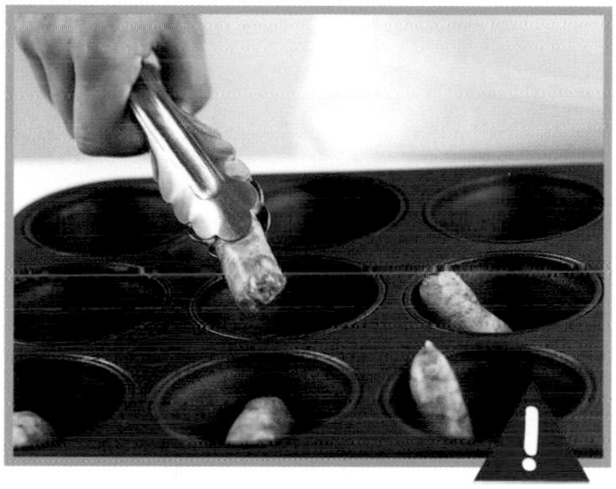

3. Add 1 tsp of oil to each muffin hole and heat the tray in the oven for 3 minutes. Take the hot tray out of the oven and add a piece of sausage to each hole.

4. Put the tray back into the oven for 4 minutes. Remove the tray and half-fill each hole with batter. Put it back in the oven and cook for 18–20 minutes.

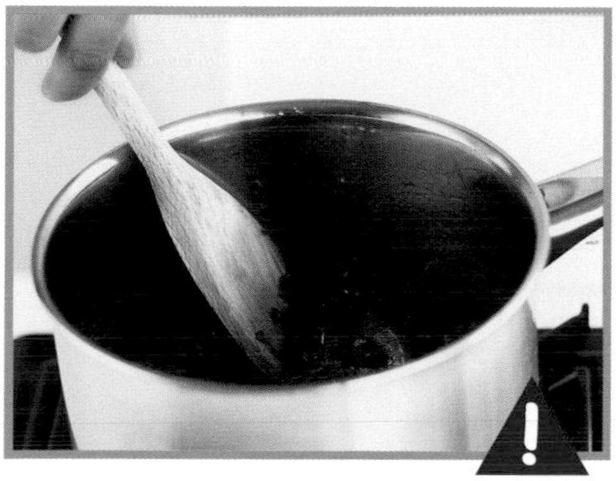

5. Meanwhile, heat the oil in the saucepan and stir in the onion, sugar, and vinegar. Gently cook the onion for 10 minutes until soft and browned.

6. Spoon the onion out of the pan onto a plate and melt the butter in the same pan. Add the flour and stir for 30 seconds, or until browned.

7. Add the stock and bring it to a boil. Boil for 1 minute, and then add the onion. Lower the heat and then **simmer** for 10 minutes, or until thickened.

hard 3 • **preparation** 25–30 minutes • **cooking** 1 hour 20 minutes

Roast chicken

Everyone loves an old-fashioned roast chicken dinner! With this easy-to-follow recipe, you can produce a meal to be proud of. Make sure you read the recipe carefully and the chicken is cooked properly in Steps 5 and 6. See p.123 for advice on how to check if your meat is cooked.

Tools

- ❑ paper towels
- ❑ cutting board
- ❑ small mixing bowl
- ❑ 2 dessert spoons
- ❑ string
- ❑ sharp knife
- ❑ roasting pan
- ❑ oven mitts
- ❑ rack
- ❑ tray
- ❑ carving knife
- ❑ carving fork

Ingredients for 4 servings

Recipe idea

Serve your roast chicken with mashed potatoes (see p.64–65) and your favorite vegetables, such as peas and carrots. It also tastes great with a splash of gravy. Use the recipe from p.74–75 or store-bought gravy mix.

3-lb whole chicken

1 lemon + 1 tsp zest

⅓ cup unsalted butter (softened)

salt and pepper

1 Tbsp fresh thyme leaves + 2 extra sprigs

To serve

mashed potatoes

1½ cups peas

2 carrots

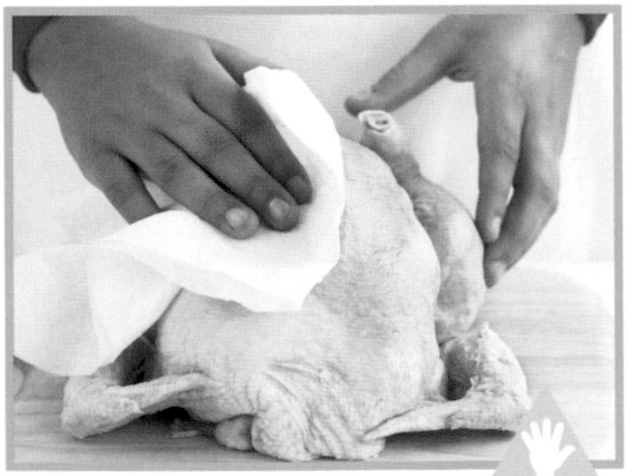

1. Preheat the oven to 400°F. Rinse inside the chicken with cold water. Place it on a board and pat it dry, inside and out, with paper towels.

2. To make the stuffing, **mix** the softened butter with the thyme leaves, lemon zest, salt, and pepper in a bowl until it forms a smooth mixture.

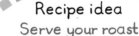

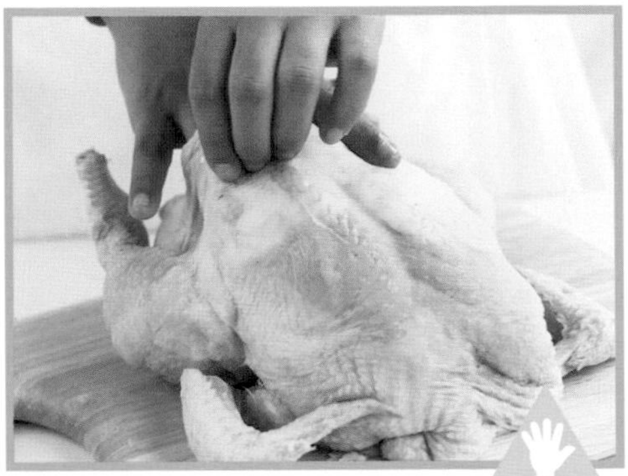

3. Lift the skin at the top of the breastbone and slide your hand in to form pockets on either side. Stuff half of the flavored butter into each pocket.

Chef's tip
Tying the chicken's legs together in Step 4 helps the chicken to keep its shape during cooking. You should also tuck the wing tips underneath.

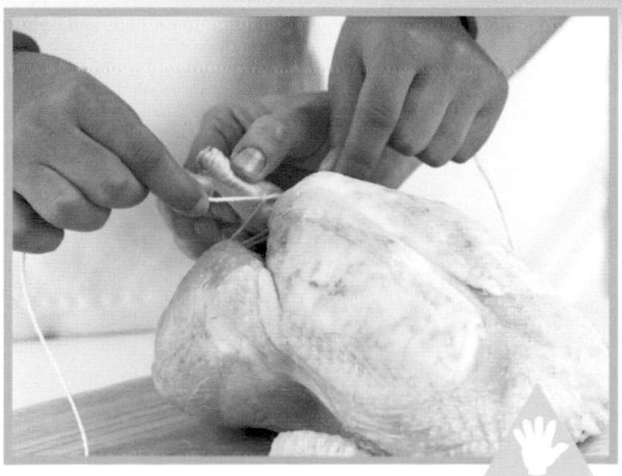

4. Cut the lemon in half. Place one half inside the chicken, with the thyme sprigs. Tie the legs together with string and put the chicken into a roasting pan.

5. Season the chicken and **roast** it for 1 hour 20 minutes, or until golden brown. **Baste** the meat after 30 minutes and then every 15 minutes after that.

6. Carefully transfer the cooked chicken to a rack (over a tray to catch any drips) and leave to rest for 10–15 minutes before carving and serving.

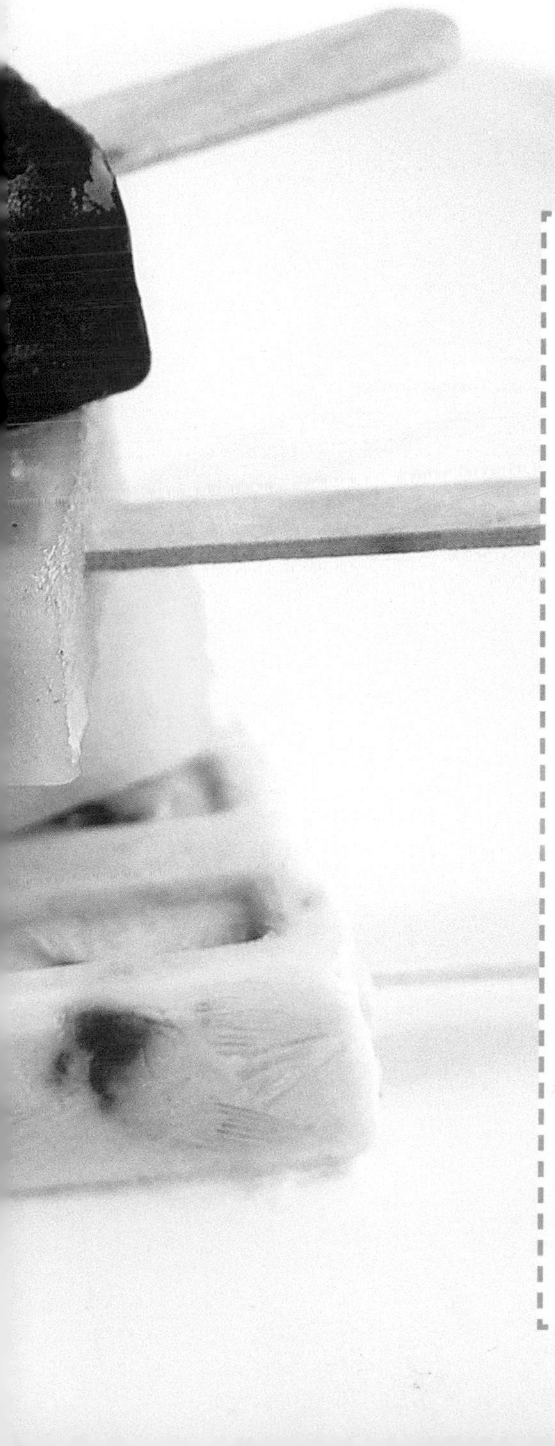

Desserts

The desserts in this section have been specially created so that they taste great and provide lots of essential nutrients. Desserts containing milk and other dairy products are good sources of protein and an important mineral called calcium, while fruit-based desserts supply vitamins and minerals.

This section introduces you to some new techniques, from whipping and whisking to melting and meringue-making. Don't forget to read the recipes thoroughly before you begin, and check out the glossary on p.122–125 for tips.

easy 1 • **preparation** 20 minutes • **freezing** 4 hours or overnight • **cooking** none

Frozen yogurt

You can use your favorite flavors to make this alternative to ice cream. What a great way to cool down on a hot summer day!

Ingredients for 8–10 scoops

⅔ cup heavy cream

¼ cup confectioner's sugar

2 cups plain yogurt

3 medium-sized chocolate cookies

½ cup soft fudge

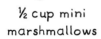

½ cup mini marshmallows

½ cup sponge candy (optional)

Tools

- ☐ cutting board
- ☐ sharp knife
- ☐ mixing bowl
- ☐ sieve
- ☐ whisk
- ☐ spatula or metal spoon
- ☐ 2 plastic tubs with lids

Recipe idea

This recipe can be made with 2 cups of your favorite ingredients, e.g., bananas, strawberries, chopped candy bars, chocolate chips, or meringues (see p.92–93).

1. Carefully **chop** the fudge and sponge candy into tiny pieces and break the cookies into slightly larger pieces. Leave to one side.

2. Pour the cream into the mixing bowl and **sift** in the confectioner's sugar. Lightly **whip** the cream to soft peaks. (Use an electric mixer or whisk.)

3. Gently **fold** the yogurt, sponge candy, fudge, cookies, and marshmallows into the cream using a plastic spatula or metal spoon.

4. Spoon the mixture into the tubs, cover, and freeze. Stir the mixture after 2 hours to prevent ice crystals from forming and freeze for at least 2 hours more.

Serving tip
When the mixture is completely frozen, allow it to soften for a few minutes before serving. Scoop out and serve in wafer cones or in bowls. Do not re-freeze.

easy 1 • **preparation** 20 minutes • **freezing** 3-4 hours • **cooking** none

Fruit pops

Make your own delicious frozen fruit pops with this simple mix-and-match recipe. Create colorful combinations with layers of fruit, yogurt, and pure juice. These fruit pops are an excellent source of vitamins, and they're a great way to cool down on a hot summer day!

Tools

- ❑ knife
- ❑ cutting board
- ❑ food processor
- ❑ sieve
- ❑ wooden spoon
- ❑ 2 mixing bowls
- ❑ 6 fruit pop molds
- ❑ 6 fruit pop sticks
- ❑ teaspoon

Ingredients for 6 lollipops

Recipe idea
Any of your favorite fruits or fruit juices would taste great in this recipe. Stir ⅔ cup strawberries into 1 cup of flavored yogurt to make 4 creamy fruit pops.

2 cups strawberries

1¼ cup orange juice

3 large kiwi fruits

3 Tbsp confectioner's sugar

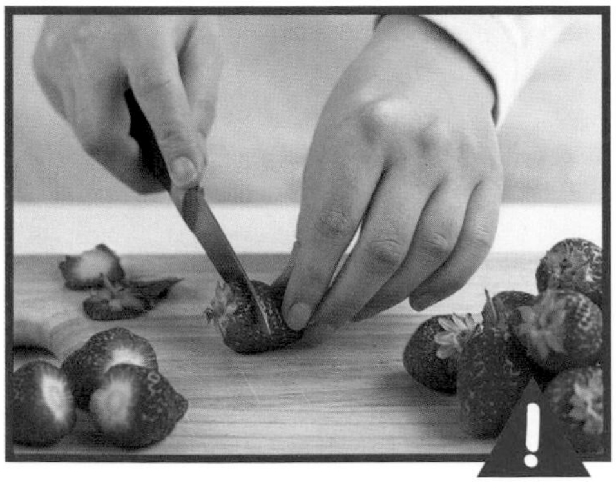

1. First, rinse and drain the strawberries in cold water. **Hull** and quarter the strawberries and then put them in the food processor.

2. Cut a thin slice off the top and bottom of each kiwi fruit. Working from top to bottom, carefully **slice** the skins off and then roughly chop the kiwis.

3. In a food processor, **blend** the strawberries with 1 Tbsp of the confectioner's sugar. **Strain** the purée into a bowl and throw away the seeds.

Serving tip
If you have any problems getting the fruit pops out of the molds, run them under the faucet.

4. Wash the food processor and sieve. Blend the kiwi fruit with 2 Tbsp of confectioner's sugar. Strain the kiwi purée into a bowl and throw away the seeds.

5. Add the first layer and freeze for 1 hour to set. Add the next layer and push the stick gently into the first layer. Freeze for 1 hour and add the last layer.

6. Do not fill the molds to the top, since the mixture will expand a little as it freezes. Freeze the fruit pops for a final 1–2 hours before eating.

easy 1 • **preparation** 20 minutes • **chilling** 2 hours • **cooking** 5 minutes

No-bake chocolate cake

This cake looks great, but it's actually very simple because, unlike most cakes, it doesn't involve any baking! It is a tempting mixture of melt-in-your-mouth chocolate, crumbly cookies, chewy cherries, and crunchy nuts.

Tools

- ❑ 1 lb loaf tin
- ❑ plastic wrap
- ❑ 2 medium mixing bowls
- ❑ small saucepan
- ❑ wooden spoon
- ❑ cutting board
- ❑ sharp knife
- ❑ oven mitts
- ❑ rubber spoon spatula
- ❑ dessert spoon

Ingredients for 10–12 servings

1 cup semisweet chocolate

1 cup unsalted butter

1 Tbsp honey

10 plain cookies

½ cup red glacé cherries (optional)

½ cup shelled pistachio nuts (optional)

⅓ cup raisins (optional)

¼ cup blanched almonds (optional)

Recipe idea

You can miss out the cherries, raisins, and nuts, if you like, and replace them with other dried fruits, marshmallows, or puffed rice.

1. Tear off a piece of plastic wrap at least twice the size of the loaf pan. Loosely **line** the pan with the plastic wrap and then set the pan to one side.

2. Break the chocolate into a bowl and add the butter and honey. Place the bowl over a pan of barely simmering water and gently **melt** the contents.

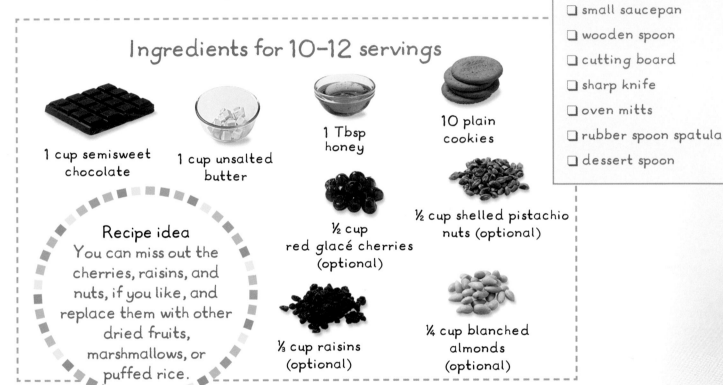

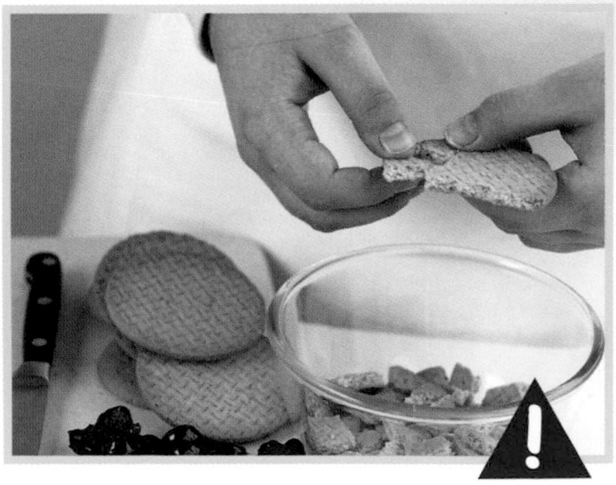

3. Halve the cherries and break the cookies into small pieces. If you would prefer a smoother cake, break the cookies into even smaller pieces.

When the cake has softened, cut it into 10–12 equal slices.

4. Using oven mitts, remove the chocolate from the heat, and allow the bowl to cool slightly. Stir in the remaining ingredients until coated.

5. Spoon the mixture into the pan and press down with the back of a spoon. Loosely cover with the extra plastic wrap and chill for 2 hours, to set.

6. Carefully turn the pan upside down on a cutting board. Remove the pan and unwrap the plastic. Let the cake soften for a few minutes.

medium 2

• **preparation** 40 minutes • **chilling** 2½–3½ hours or overnight • **cooking** about 5 minutes

Mandarin cheesecake

This scrumptious cheesecake looks amazing but is simple to make. The filling is a mixture of cream cheese, condensed milk, and lemon juice, and the base is just made of crushed graham crackers and a little melted butter. Best of all, this cheesecake does not need any baking, just chilling.

Tools

- ☐ plastic food bag
- ☐ rolling pin
- ☐ wooden spoon
- ☐ medium saucepan
- ☐ 8-inch flan pan (loose-bottomed and fluted)
- ☐ measuring spoon
- ☐ mixing bowl
- ☐ balloon whisk
- ☐ colander
- ☐ knife
- ☐ cutting board
- ☐ baking tray
- ☐ rubber spoon spatula

Ingredients for 8–10 servings

15 graham cracker rectangles

⅓ cup unsalted butter

¾ cup cream cheese, at room temperature

10-oz sweetened condensed milk

5 Tbsp fresh lemon juice

10-oz can mandarin orange segments in juice

Recipe idea

Other canned fruits would taste great in this recipe. Try cherries, peaches, pineapple, or a combination of your favorite fruits.

1. Break up the crackers and put them into a food bag. Push the air out and seal. **Crush** the crackers with a rolling pin until they are like fine breadcrumbs.

2. Gently **melt** the butter in a saucepan, over a low heat. Turn off the heat and stir in the crushed crackers until they are completely coated with butter.

3. Put the flan pan on a baking tray and pour in the cracker mixture. Spread the mixture out with the back of a spoon until it evenly covers the base and sides.

Chef's tip
For an extra-special dessert, sprinkle some grated chocolate on top of the cheesecake.

4. Chill the cracker base for 30 minutes. **Beat** the cream cheese and then add the condensed milk and lemon juice. **Whisk** them all together, until smooth.

5. Thoroughly drain the mandarin orange segments and roughly chop them into smaller pieces. Scatter them over the chilled cracker base.

6. Pour the filling mixture over the base. Use a spatula to spread the mixture and smooth the top. Chill for 2–3 hours or overnight to set.

medium 2 • **preparation** 20 minutes • **cooking** none

Summer fruit ripple

This creamy, light dessert looks great and tastes delicious! Although this recipe suggests fresh fruit, frozen fruit would be fine, but you must thaw it completely before you begin. On a hot summer day, you can freeze the finished ripple for at least 4 hours to make a super-cool treat.

Tools

- ❑ chopping board
- ❑ sharp knife
- ❑ food processor
- ❑ sieve
- ❑ 2 mixing bowls
- ❑ wooden spoon
- ❑ dessert spoon
- ❑ balloon whisk
- ❑ metal mixing spoon
- ❑ rubber spoon spatula

Ingredients for 4 servings

2 cups ripe strawberries

1 cup ripe raspberries

1 cup ripe blueberries

4 Tbsp fresh orange juice

1 cup plain yogurt

1 cup heavy cream

2 Tbsp honey

2 Tbsp confectioner's sugar (sifted)

Recipe idea

Try using canned fruit such as mangoes and peaches, but remember to set some fruit aside for decoration.

1. Wash all the fruit and put a handful to one side (They will be used to decorate the finished dessert.) **Hull** the strawberries and cut them in quarters.

2. Place the orange juice, sugar, and half of the fruit into the food processor. Put the lid on securely and **blend** until they are a smooth purée.

3. **Strain** the blended fruit over a mixing bowl to separate the seeds and fruit pulp. Use a wooden spoon to press the liquid through.

If you don't have a food processor, use a masher to crush the fruit in Step 2.

Serving tip
Finally, place the reserved fruit from Step 1 on top of the rippled mixture in the serving glasses.

4. Carefully stir the rest of the strawberries, blueberries, and raspberries into the fruit purée with a metal spoon (excluding the fruit set aside in Step 1).

5. Lightly **whip** the cream in the large bowl. When it is ready, it will stand up in soft peaks. (You can use an electric mixer if you have one.)

6. **Fold** the yogurt, honey, and half of the fruit mixture into the cream. Layer the marbled cream mixture with the rest of the fruit mixture in serving glasses.

Fruit crisp

A crisp is a baked fruit dessert with a crunchy oat topping. It tastes great served with ice cream or whipped cream. Like all fruits, blackberries and peaches are a good source of vitamins, while the oats used in the crisp topping provide carbohydrates.

Tools

- ❑ cutting board
- ❑ sharp knife
- ❑ teaspoon
- ❑ 2 mixing bowls
- ❑ metal mixing spoon
- ❑ wooden spoon
- ❑ sieve
- ❑ baking tray
- ❑ oven mitts
- ❑ ovenproof dish (approx. 9 x 6 in and 2 in deep)

Ingredients for 4-6 servings

4 large ripe peaches (or 6 small ones)

2 cups ripe blackberries

¼ cup light brown sugar

2-3 pinches ground cinnamon

For the topping

1 cup flour

1½ cups jumbo rolled oats

½ cup light brown sugar

⅔ cup unsalted butter (diced)

Recipe idea
Other fruits such as raspberries, apples, plums, or blueberries would taste great in this recipe.

1. Preheat the oven to 375°F. Cut around each peach and twist them so that they split in half. Scoop the stones out with a teaspoon.

2. Slice the halved peaches in half again and then **chop** each piece into three more chunks. Rinse and thoroughly drain the blackberries.

3. Mix the sugar and cinnamon together in a bowl. **Fold** in the peaches and blackberries until they are completely coated in the sugar mixture.

If your fruit is not ripe, you may need to add more sugar in Step 3.

Safety tip
Leave the crisp to stand for 10 minutes before serving. It will still be warm but cool enough to eat!

4. **Sift** the flour into a separate bowl and stir in the brown sugar. Add the oats to the bowl and stir them into the flour and sugar.

5. Using your fingertips, **rub** the diced butter into the flour mixture. The mixture should come together in small lumps when it is ready.

6. Place the dish on a baking tray and spoon in the fruit filling. Scatter the topping over and **bake** the crisp for 30 minutes or until golden.

• **preparation** 40–45 minutes • **cooking** 2 hours

Tropical fruit meringues

Here's a handy tip—egg whites are easier to whisk when they are at room temperature. You should also use a clean, grease-free glass bowl when making meringues, and make sure the whites are completely free of any yolk.

Tools

- ❑ baking sheet
- ❑ nonstick parchment paper
- ❑ large bowl
- ❑ electric mixer
- ❑ tablespoon
- ❑ metal mixing spoon
- ❑ 2 dessert spoons
- ❑ cutting board
- ❑ sharp knife
- ❑ large mixing bowl
- ❑ oven mitts

Add some meringue pieces in Step 6 of the Fruit Ripple on p.88–89.

Ingredients for 12 meringues

2 eggs

½ cup sugar

1 pinch of salt

For the fruit salad

½ small melon (quartered and deseeded)

1 kiwi fruit

2 Tbsp fresh orange juice

1 small mango

10 red grapes (halved)

10 green grapes (halved)

½ small pineapple

Recipe idea
You can use any of your favorite fruits in the salad—apple, peach, or banana would all taste great.

Chef's tip
Cooked meringues will be dry and should peel off the parchment very easily.

1. Preheat the oven to 225°F and line a baking sheet with nonstick parchment paper. **Separate** the egg whites from the yolks. (See p.125 for tips.)

2. **Whisk** the egg whites and salt in a large bowl, until they form stiff peaks. Whisk 5 Tbsp of the sugar into the mixture, 1 Tbsp at a time.

3. Make sure the egg whites are stiff before adding each tablespoon of sugar. **Fold** the remaining sugar into the mixture, using a metal spoon.

4. Using 2 dessert spoons, put 12 spoonfuls of the meringue onto the baking sheet and bake on the bottom shelf of the oven for 2 hours.

5. Carefully slice the mango in half, around the stone. **Slice** the skin from the melon. Scoop out the mango and melon flesh and cut them into cubes.

6. Prepare the pineapple and kiwi. First cut off the top and bottom and then slice off the skin, working downward. Cut out the core from the pineapple.

7. Cut the kiwi into slices and the pineapple into cubes. Mix all the fruit together and stir in the orange juice. Chill until the meringues are ready.

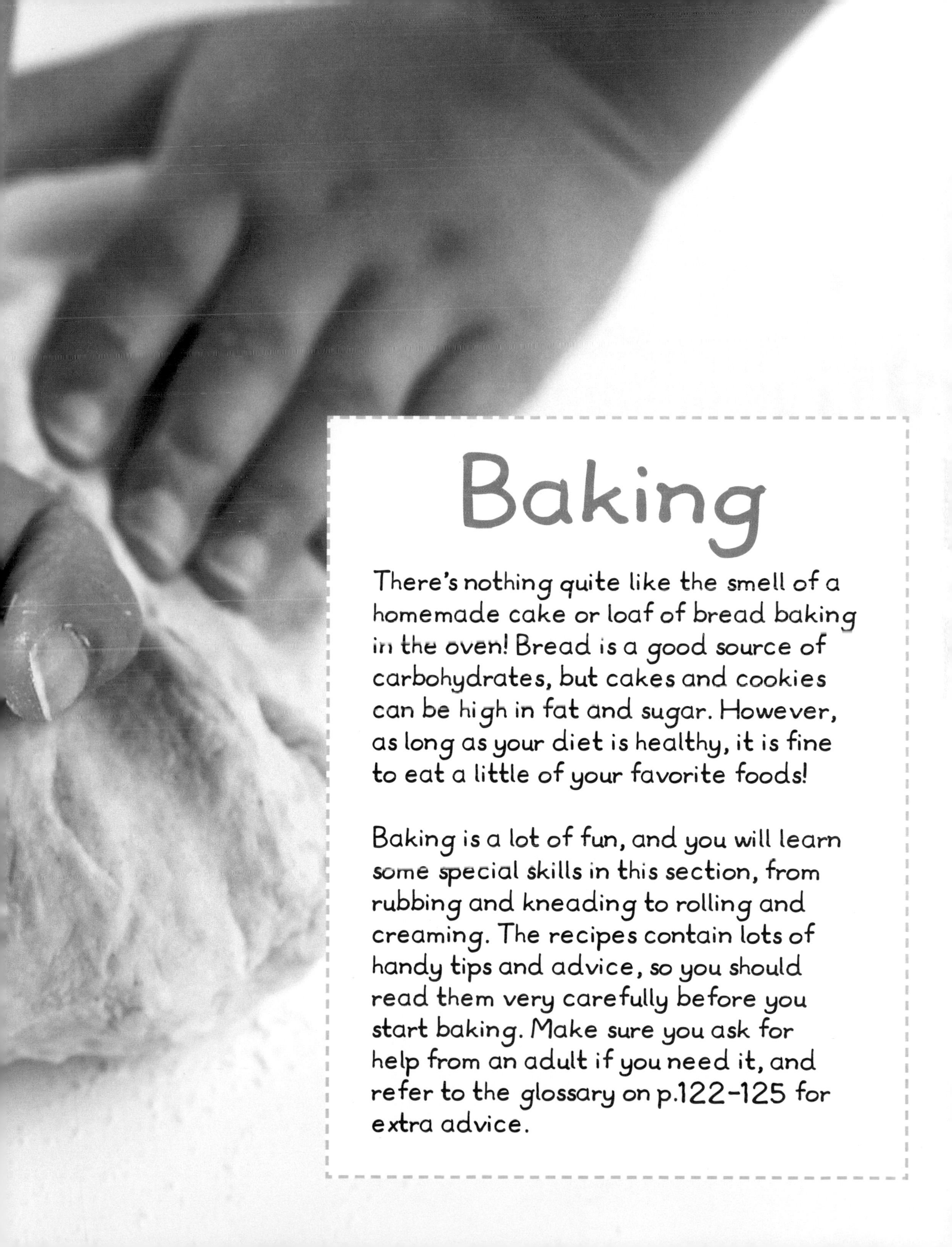

Baking

There's nothing quite like the smell of a homemade cake or loaf of bread baking in the oven! Bread is a good source of carbohydrates, but cakes and cookies can be high in fat and sugar. However, as long as your diet is healthy, it is fine to eat a little of your favorite foods!

Baking is a lot of fun, and you will learn some special skills in this section, from rubbing and kneading to rolling and creaming. The recipes contain lots of handy tips and advice, so you should read them very carefully before you start baking. Make sure you ask for help from an adult if you need it, and refer to the glossary on p.122–125 for extra advice.

medium 2

• **preparation** 30–35 minutes • **cooking** 25 minutes

Crunchy muffins

The secret to delicious, light muffins is to not overmix the batter. A few lumps don't matter—but if the batter is overmixed, the muffins will have a heavy, dense texture.

Tools

- ❑ sieve
- ❑ wooden spoon
- ❑ mixing bowl
- ❑ whisk
- ❑ measuring cup
- ❑ metal mixing spoon
- ❑ 12 paper muffin liners
- ❑ 12-cup muffin tin
- ❑ tablespoon
- ❑ teaspoon
- ❑ oven mitts
- ❑ cooling rack

Ingredients for 12 muffins

1⅓ cups flour

1 Tbsp baking powder

½ tsp salt

½ cup sugar

1 egg

2 Tbsp corn oil or sunflower oil

1 cup milk

1 cup granola

1 cup fresh raspberries

1 cup white chocolate (chopped)

Recipe idea

Frozen raspberries would be fine for this recipe, as long as you thaw them completely. Try other fresh or frozen fruits, such as strawberries, blueberries, or blackberries. Nuts, dried fruit, or chocolate chips would also taste great!

1. Preheat the oven to 400°F. **Sift** the flour, baking powder, and salt into a mixing bowl. Stir the sugar into the sifted mixture.

2. **Crack** the egg into a measuring cup and add the oil. **Beat** the egg and oil together. Add the milk and then **whisk** the mixture.

3. **Fold** the egg mixture into the flour mixture. The mixture will be lumpy, but no flour should be visible. Then fold in the chocolate and raspberries.

Don't worry if the raspberries break up in Step 3. The muffins will still taste delicious!

4. Put the muffin liners into the muffin tray and spoon the mixture into them. The easiest way is with a tablespoon and the back of a teaspoon.

5. Sprinkle some of the granola on top of each muffin. Bake them in the oven for 25 minutes, or until the muffins are risen and golden.

6. Remove the muffins from the oven and allow them to cool in the muffin tin before placing them on a cooling rack. Then you can help yourself!

Chocolate brownies

Here are a few tips for baking brownies: Melt the chocolate over low heat and make sure the bowl does not touch the water in the pan. You must fold, not stir, the mixture in Step 5, and you should always line the tin to prevent the brownies from sticking to it.

Tools

- ❑ 8-x-6-in brownie pan
- ❑ scissors
- ❑ pencil
- ❑ nonstick parchment paper
- ❑ 3 medium bowls
- ❑ wooden spoon
- ❑ small saucepan
- ❑ sieve
- ❑ rubber spoon spatula
- ❑ palette knife
- ❑ oven mitts

Ingredients for 12-16 brownies

3 oz semisweet chocolate

⅔ cup unsalted butter + extra for greasing

1 cup flour

1 Tbsp cocoa powder

½ tsp baking powder

1 tsp vanilla extract

¾ cup soft light brown sugar

1 pinch of salt

2 eggs

⅔ cup chopped pecans (optional)

Recipe idea

If you don't like nuts or are allergic to them, you can leave them out. These brownies taste just as delicious without nuts.

1. Preheat the oven to 350°F. **Grease** and **line** the base of the brownie pan with nonstick parchment paper. (See p.124 for hints and tips on this.)

2. Break the chocolate into a bowl and add the butter. **Melt** the butter and chocolate over a saucepan of barely simmering water, stirring occasionally.

3. Remove the bowl from the heat and allow the chocolate to cool slightly. **Sift** the flour, cocoa powder, baking powder, and salt into a separate bowl.

Chef's tip
A brownie should be firm on the outside but gooey and fudgelike on the inside.

4. In a third bowl, **beat** the eggs and then add the sugar and vanilla extract. **Stir** the ingredients together until they are just combined.

5. **Fold** the melted chocolate into the beaten egg mixture. Then fold in the flour mixture and nuts. There should be no visible flour.

6. Spoon the mixture into the pan, smooth the top with a palette knife, and bake for 25 minutes. Allow it to cool in the pan before cutting into squares.

medium 2 • **preparation** 35 minutes • **cooking** about 45 minutes

Chocolate cookies

This is a versatile recipe for melt-in-your-mouth cookies. You can use either chocolate spread for a double chocolate taste, or peanut butter for a chocolate-and-nut flavor.

Tools

- ❑ 2 mixing bowls
- ❑ electric mixer
- ❑ sieve
- ❑ plastic spatula
- ❑ wooden spoon
- ❑ dessert spoon
- ❑ teaspoon
- ❑ 3 baking trays
- ❑ oven mitts
- ❑ cooling rack
- ❑ palette knife

Ingredients for 20 cookies

½ cup unsalted butter, softened

½ cup soft light brown sugar

1 egg

½ cup chocolate spread

⅓ cup cocoa powder

2–3 drops of vanilla extract

¾ cup sugar

1⅔ cups flour

1 cup white chocolate chips

1 pinch of salt

½ tsp baking powder

Recipe idea

For a nutty cookie, skip the cocoa powder in Step 3, replace the chocolate spread with the same amount of peanut butter in Step 4, and use semisweet chocolate chips instead.

1. Preheat the oven to 350°F. **Cream** the butter and sugar and brown sugar together in a large bowl until the mixture turns pale and creamy.

2. Still using the electric mixer, **beat** the egg, chocolate spread, and vanilla extract into the creamed butter and sugar mixture, until fully mixed in.

3. **Sift** the flour, baking powder, cocoa powder, and salt into a bowl. Use a wooden spoon to push the mixture through, if you need to.

Chef's tip
For best results, bake each tray of cookies separately on the middle shelf of the oven.

You can use milk, white, or semisweet chocolate chips, or even a mixture!

4. Add the sifted flour mixture to the chocolate mixture and gently **mix** them together with a wooden spoon. Stir in the chocolate chips.

5. Place 6–7 heaped tablespoons of cookie dough onto each baking tray, leaving space between each mound so they can spread as they cook.

6. Bake for 14 minutes. Take the trays out of the oven and leave the cookies to set for 2–3 minutes. When set, transfer them onto a cooling rack.

• **preparation** 30 minutes • **cooking** 35 minutes

Banana squares

The melt-in-your mouth texture of this cake is due to the creaming and folding in Steps 2 and 3 which make mixture light and airy. Adding the fresh banana and buttermilk (or yogurt) in Step 3 also makes the cake deliciously moist.

To make muffins, bake the mixture in a muffin tin for 25–30 minutes.

Tools

- ❑ pencil
- ❑ 8-inch square cake pan
- ❑ nonstick parchment paper
- ❑ scissors
- ❑ 2 large mixing bowls
- ❑ electric mixer
- ❑ sieve
- ❑ wooden spoon
- ❑ palette knife
- ❑ frying pan
- ❑ oven mitts
- ❑ wooden spatula
- ❑ plate
- ❑ cooling rack

Recipe idea
For a plain and simple cake, leave out the frosting, or try some whipped cream instead.

Ingredients for 12–16 squares

½ cup unsalted butter (softened) + extra for greasing

½ cup soft light brown sugar

2 eggs (beaten)

1¾ cups self-rising flour

1 tsp baking powder

1 pinch of salt

1 lb ripe bananas (peeled and mashed)

2 Tbsp buttermilk or plain yogurt

For the frosting (optional)

¾ cup cream cheese (room temperature)

½ cup icing sugar (sifted)

¾ cup desiccated coconut

Chef's tip
Allow the cake to cool in the pan for 5–10 minutes in Step 4 before gently turning it out on to the cooling rack.

1. Preheat the oven to 350°F. With a pencil, draw around the pan onto the parchment paper. Cut out the square. **Grease** and **line** the pan.

2. **Cream** the butter and sugar together in a large bowl until light and fluffy. Gradually beat the eggs into the creamed butter and sugar mixture.

3. **Sift** the flour, salt, and baking powder into the creamed mixture and gently **fold** to combine. Next, stir in the banana and buttermilk.

4. Spoon the cake mixture into the prepared pan and smooth the top with a palette knife. Bake the cake in the oven for 35 minutes, or until risen.

5. Meanwhile, **dry-fry** the coconut over low heat until golden, stirring continuously. Put the toasted coconut on a plate to stop it from burning.

6. **Beat** the cream cheese and confectioner's sugar together until completely combined. The mixture should become smooth, soft, and spreadable.

7. When the cake is completely cool, cut it into squares. Add a spoonful of the cream cheese topping and a sprinkling of toasted coconut to each square.

medium 2 • **preparation** 30–35 minutes • **rising** about 2½ hours • **cooking** 30–35 minutes

Homemade bread

It is simple to create a light, airy loaf of bread. All you need are a few basic ingredients—flour, yeast, salt, and water. The most important thing is to learn special bread-making skills, such as kneading and punching down. These are all explained in the glossary on p.124.

Tools

- ❑ ramekin
- ❑ sieve
- ❑ mixing bowl
- ❑ wooden spoon
- ❑ large bowl
- ❑ plastic wrap
- ❑ 2 (1 lb) loaf pans
- ❑ pastry brush
- ❑ oven mitts

Food fact

Yeast helps the bread rise and gives it a light texture.

Recipe idea

If you don't have fresh yeast, you can use 1½ tsp instant dry yeast instead. Skip Step 1 and stir the dry yeast and 1 tsp sugar into the sifted flour in Step 2.

Ingredients for 2 loaves

1 cup lukewarm water

1 Tbsp olive oil, plus extra for greasing

1 Tbsp fresh yeast

1 tsp sugar

2 tsp salt

3½ cups white bread flour, plus extra for kneading

For the topping

2 tsp poppy seeds (optional)

1 egg (beaten)

2 tsp sesame seeds (optional)

Chef's tip
The dough needs to be put in a warm, but not hot, place to rise. A place near a warm oven or radiator works well.

1. Using your finger, mix 3 Tbsp of the water with the yeast and sugar. Leave it in a warm place for 10 minutes or until it begins to bubble.

2. **Sift** the flour and salt into a bowl and stir in the yeast mixture. Stir in the oil and then enough of the remaining water to make a soft dough.

3. Lightly flour your hands and the work surface. **Knead** the dough for about 10 minutes or until it becomes smooth and elastic. (See p.124 for tips.)

4. Put the dough in a lightly greased bowl and cover it with greased plastic wrap. Put it in a warm place for 1½ hours, until the dough has doubled in size.

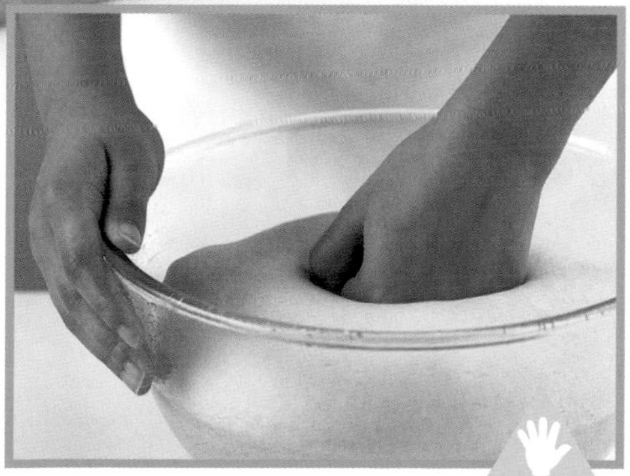

5. Preheat the oven to 425°F. Gently **punch down** the risen dough and then knead it on a lightly floured surface for 5 minutes more.

6. **Shape** the dough into 2 rectangles. Place each piece into a lightly greased loaf pan, cover, and put them in a warm place until they have doubled in size.

7. **Glaze** the loaves with egg and sprinkle with seeds. Bake for 30–35 minutes. A cooked loaf will look golden and sound hollow if tapped on the base.

• **preparation** 40-45 minutes • **rising** about 1 hour • **cooking** 4-6 minutes

Naan bread

Naan is a special type of flatbread that originated in India. Unlike the traditional bread on p.104–105, the naan bread is broiled rather than baked. As the naan cooks, a hollow pocket forms inside, which is perfect for adding a tasty filling. Naan can accompany a curry.

The dough will be sticky in Step 3, so rub a little flour on your hands.

Tools

- ❑ ramekin
- ❑ sieve
- ❑ wooden spoon
- ❑ 2 large bowls
- ❑ plastic wrap
- ❑ table knife
- ❑ rolling pin
- ❑ baking tray
- ❑ pastry brush
- ❑ oven mitts

Recipe idea
If you are using dry yeast, skip Step 1 and stir in 1 tsp of instant dry yeast in Step 2.

Ingredients for 4 naans

3 Tbsp lukewarm milk

2 tsp fresh yeast

1⅔ cups white bread flour

½ tsp table salt

2 tsp cumin seeds (optional)

1 egg (beaten)

vegetable oil (for greasing)

3 Tbsp plain yogurt

2 Tbsp unsalted butter (melted)

Chef's tip
The milk in Step 1 should be lukewarm, not hot. If it is too hot, it will kill the yeast and the bread will not rise.

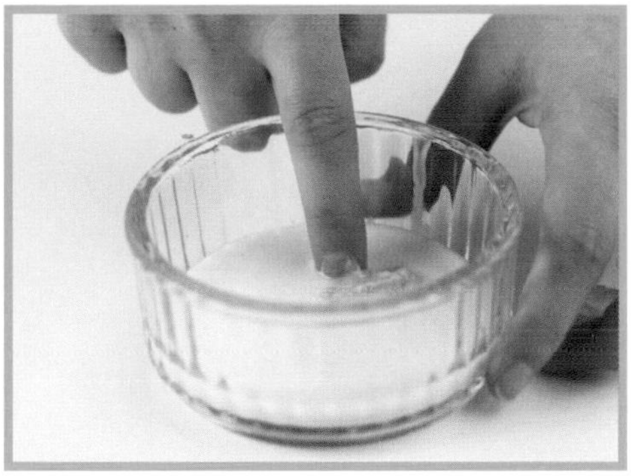

1. Using your finger, mix the milk and fresh yeast together in a ramekin. Leave the mixture in a warm place for 10 minutes or until it bubbles slightly.

2. **Sift** the flour and salt into a bowl. Using a wooden spoon, gradually stir the yeast mixture, egg, and yogurt into the flour until you have a soft dough.

3. On a lightly floured surface, **knead** the dough for 5 minutes or until it is smooth and elastic. Lightly grease a bowl with oil and then add the dough.

4. Cover the bowl with lightly greased plastic wrap and leave it in a warm place for about 1 hour or until the dough has doubled in size.

5. Remove the plastic wrap and **punch down** the dough. Divide the dough into 4 pieces and knead a quarter of the cumin seeds into each piece (optional).

6. **Roll** each piece into a teardrop shape. Don't be afraid to stretch the dough to get the right shape! Preheat the baking tray under a hot broiler.

7. Place the naans on the hot baking tray and **glaze** both sides with melted butter. **Broil** on high for 2–3 minutes on each side or until risen and golden.

hard 3 • **preparation** 60 minutes • **rising** 1–1½ hours • **cooking** 20–25 minutes

Pizza

The pizza base is made in the same way as the bread on p.104–105. However, the dough only needs to rise once in this recipe, rather than twice, like the bread.

Tools

- ❑ ramekin
- ❑ 2 sieves
- ❑ mixing bowl
- ❑ 2 wooden spoons
- ❑ large bowl
- ❑ plastic wrap
- ❑ small bowl
- ❑ small saucepan
- ❑ teaspoon
- ❑ cutting board
- ❑ rolling pin
- ❑ baking tray
- ❑ dessert spoon
- ❑ oven mitts

Ingredients for 2 pizzas

For the base

2 cups flour

⅔ cup water

1 tsp fresh yeast

1 tsp sugar

1 Tbsp olive oil + extra for greasing

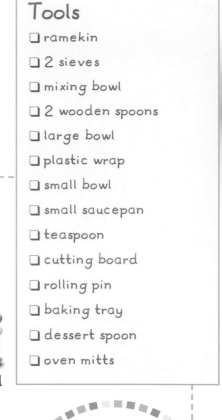

½ tsp salt

For the topping

1 small can chopped tomatoes

1 Tbsp tomato paste

salt and pepper

1 tsp dried oregano

2 slices ham

1 small can pineapple pieces

1 ball mozzarella (sliced and drained)

Recipe idea
Experiment with other toppings, such as pepperoni, mushrooms, onions, peppers, or anchovies.

1. To make the base, follow Steps 1–4 on p.104–105. While the dough is rising in Step 4, use a sieve to drain the excess liquid from the tomatoes.

2. Put the tomatoes into a small saucepan and add the tomato paste, oregano, salt, and pepper. Gently **warm** them over low heat for 2 minutes.

3. With your fingers, tear the ham and mozzarella into bite-sized pieces. Drain the pineapple pieces. Preheat the oven to 425°F.

Pesto is a tasty alternative to tomato sauce on a pizza. (See p. 38–39 for a recipe.)

Chef's tip
To prevent sticking and make equal-sized circles in Step 4, turn the dough 45° after each roll.

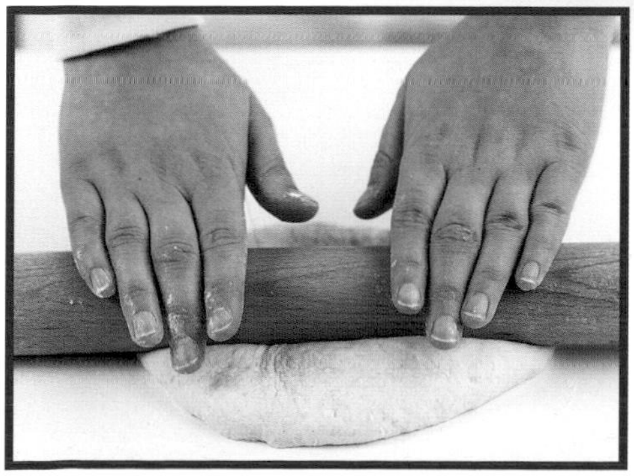

4. **Punch down** the dough and put it on a lightly floured work surface. **Roll** it out into 2 equal-sized circles, about 6 in in diameter.

5. Place the pizza bases on a lightly greased baking tray. Spread half of the tomato sauce onto each base, leaving a ¾-in rim around the edge.

6. Add the toppings and bake the pizzas for 20–25 minutes. Let the pizzas cool a little before cutting and eating, since the cheese will be very hot!

• **preparation** 30 minutes • **chilling** 15 minutes • **cooking** 20 minutes

Strawberry shortcakes

These strawberry shortcakes are a perfect way to impress your family and friends. You can bake them in advance and store them in an airtight container. When you are ready, whip up the toppings and serve the shortcakes.

Tools

- ❑ mixing bowl
- ❑ electric mixer
- ❑ fork
- ❑ sieve
- ❑ plastic wrap
- ❑ rolling pin
- ❑ parchment paper
- ❑ cookie cutter
- ❑ large baking sheet
- ❑ small saucepan
- ❑ measuring spoons
- ❑ oven mitts
- ❑ cooling rack

Ingredients for 12 shortcakes

½ cup unsalted butter, softened + extra for greasing

⅓ cup sugar

1 cup flour

½ cup corn starch

For the topping

1½ cups strawberries (hulled and quartered)

3 Tbsp raspberry jam

1¼ cups heavy cream (whipped)

Recipe tip

Experiment with other fruit toppings, such as blueberries, blackberries, or raspberries. Or add 1 tsp of orange zest to the biscuit mixture in Step 2 and serve without the topping.

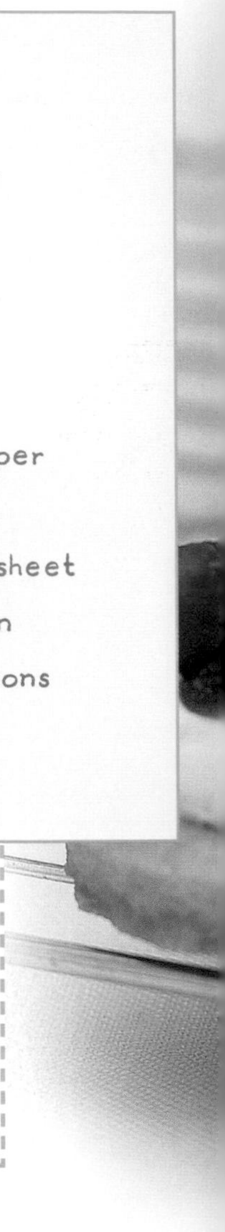

1. Preheat the oven to 325°F. Place the butter and sugar in a bowl and **cream** together until light and fluffy using an electric mixer.

2. **Sift** the plain flour and corn starch into the creamed butter. **Mix** together with a fork until all the ingredients are combined.

3. Form the dough into a smooth, round disc, using your hands. Wrap the dough in plastic wrap and chill it in the refrigerator for 15 minutes.

Experiment with different cookie cutter shapes, like hearts, flowers, or stars.

Serving tip
Add a generous dollop of whipped cream to each biscuit and top with a spoonful of the strawberries.

4. Place the chilled dough between 2 pieces of parchment paper. **Roll** it out to form a circle that is about 8 inches in diameter and ½ inch thick.

5. Cut out 12 shortbreads and place them onto a greased baking sheet. (You will need to gather and reroll the dough a few times.) Bake for 20 minutes.

6. In a pan **warm** the jam, fold in the strawberries, and leave to cool. Take the shortcakes out of the oven and allow them to set in the tray. Put them onto a rack.

hard 3 • **preparation** 15 minutes • **chilling** 1½ hours • **cooking** 7–9 minutes

Orange crunch cookies

These tangy cookies just melt in your mouth! They can be served with icing for a tasty treat, or plain for a simple homemade snack.

If you don't have a piping bag, use a spoon to drizzle the icing.

Tools

- ❑ sieve
- ❑ table knife
- ❑ 2 mixing bowls
- ❑ plastic wrap
- ❑ knife
- ❑ oven mitts
- ❑ 2 baking sheets
- ❑ cooling rack
- ❑ wooden spoon
- ❑ piping bag and nozzle, or teaspoon

Ingredients for 20–24 cookies

1 cup self-rising flour

¼ cup unsalted butter (diced) + extra for greasing

⅓ cup soft dark brown sugar

1 tsp orange zest

½ egg yolk (beaten)

1 Tbsp honey

For the icing

1 cup confectioner's sugar (sifted)

3 Tbsp fresh orange juice

Recipe idea

Try using lemon zest or ground ginger instead of orange for a tasty alternative, and use water instead of juice to make the icing.

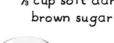

1. Preheat the oven to 350°F. **Sift** the flour into a bowl and **rub** the diced butter into the flour, until you have a breadcrumb texture.

2. Using a table knife, stir the sugar, orange zest, honey, and egg into the flour and butter, until the mixture starts to come together in lumps.

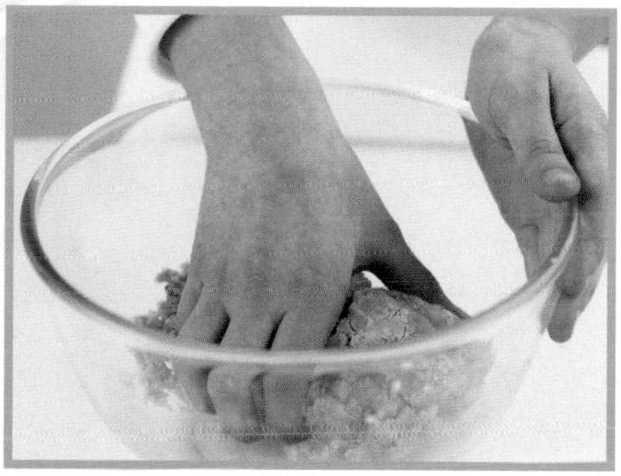

3. Use your hands to bring the lumps together to form a smooth ball of dough. Briefly knead the dough and then lightly flour the work surface.

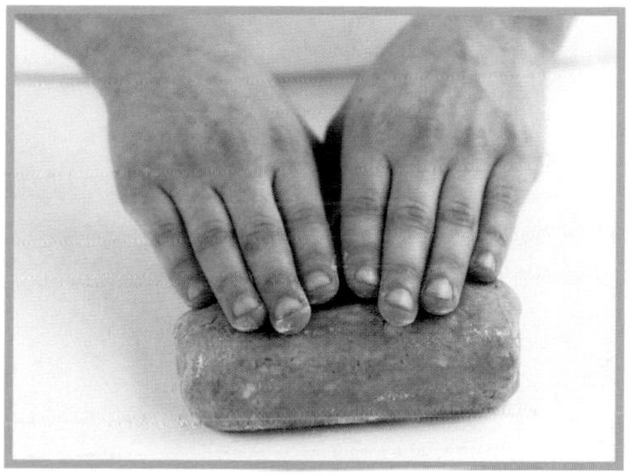

4. Roll the dough into a log, about 2 in in diameter and 4 in long. Wrap the log in plastic wrap and chill it for 1½ hours, or until firm.

Chef's tip

When slicing the dough in Step 5, rotate the roll 90° after each slice. This will help keep the cookies round. If the dough breaks, just reshape it.

5. Lightly **grease** 2 baking sheets with butter. **Slice** the log into 20–24 thin discs and place the cookies on the baking sheets. Bake for 7–9 minutes.

6. Carefully remove the cookies from the oven and allow to set and cool. **Beat** the sugar and orange juice together in a bowl to form a smooth paste.

7. Carefully transfer the cookies to a cooling rack. Put the icing into a piping bag and then **drizzle** it over the cookies in your favorite patterns.

Vegetable tart

This is a simple introduction to making savory shortcrust pastry. Here's a good tip—when making savory or sweet pastry, make sure that your hands are not too hot and the butter and water are cool to give the pastry a lighter texture.

The technique used in Step 6 is called baking blind.

Tools

- ❑ sieve
- ❑ mixing bowl
- ❑ fork
- ❑ teaspoon
- ❑ plastic wrap
- ❑ flan pan, loose-bottomed and fluted (approx. 8 in in diameter)
- ❑ rolling pin
- ❑ table knife
- ❑ baking beans or dried kidney beans
- ❑ parchment paper
- ❑ whisk
- ❑ measuring cup
- ❑ oven mitts

Recipe idea

Other fillings such as bacon, peppers, broccoli, onions, or mushrooms would taste great in this recipe.

Ingredients for 1 tart

1¾ cups plain flour + extra for rolling

1 pinch salt

2 Tbsp water

4 Tbsp unsalted butter (diced)

⅓ cup shortening (diced)

For the filling

2 eggs (beaten)

¾ cup peas

2 Tbsp cheese (grated)

½ cup cream

2 slices ham (cubed)

1 small leek (sautéed)

¾ cup corn

½ cup milk

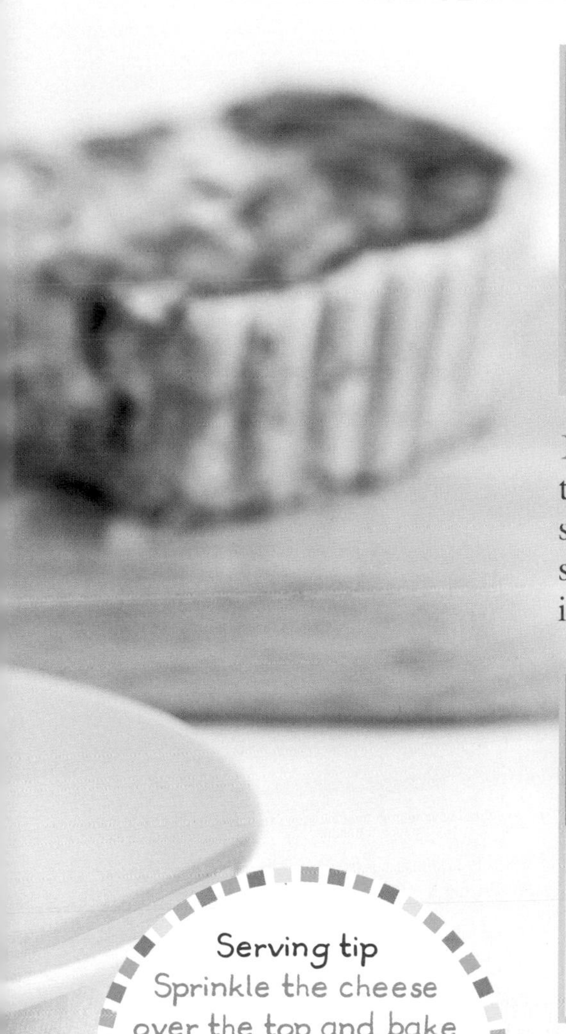

Serving tip
Sprinkle the cheese over the top and bake the tart for 45 minutes. Allow the tart to set and cool before serving.

1. **Sift** the flour and salt into the bowl. Using a fork, gently stir the diced butter and shortening into the flour until it is completely coated.

2. With your fingertips, **rub** the butter and shortening into the flour until it looks like coarse breadcrumbs. Preheat the oven to 400°F.

3. Add the water, drop by drop, and stir it into the crumbs with a table knife. When the crumbs start to stick together in lumps, gather the pastry in your hands.

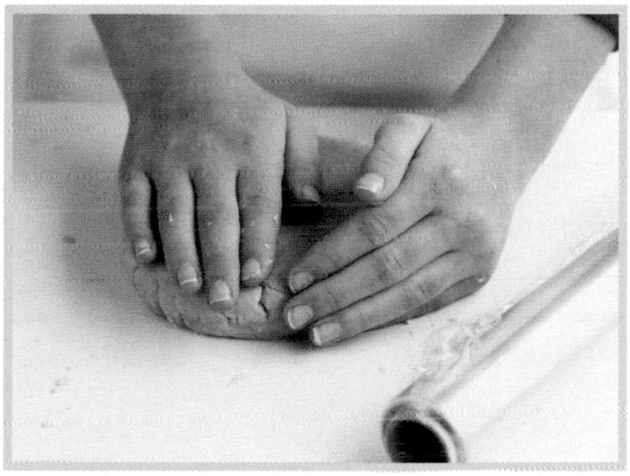

4. Shape the pastry into a smooth disc and cover it in plastic wrap. Chill it for 1 hour, or until firm. Lightly flour the work surface.

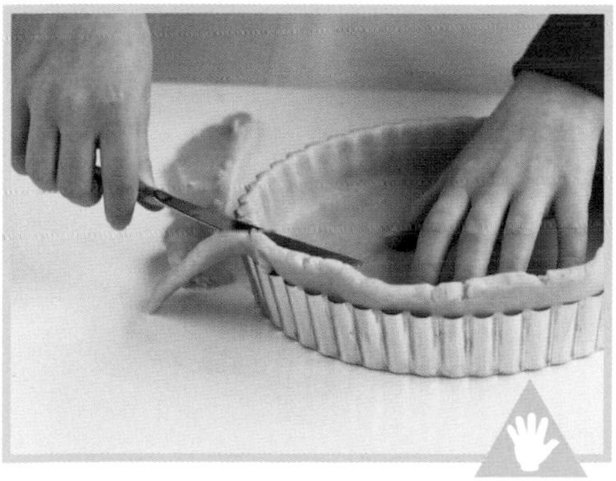

5. **Roll** out the pastry so that it is slightly bigger than the pan. Gently press it into the pan and trim off the excess. Prick the base and chill it for 15 minutes.

6. Cover the tart with 2 layers of greaseproof paper and add the baking beans. Bake for 15 minutes, remove the paper and beans, and bake for 5 minutes.

7. Reduce the oven to 350°F. Scatter the ham, peas, leeks, and corn over the base. **Whisk** the eggs, milk, and cream together and pour into the tart.

hard 3

- **preparation** 1 hour 15 minutes
- **chilling** 1 hour
- **cooking** 30-35 minutes

Apple pie

When making a pie, it's important to make a hole in the top of the pastry before you bake it—this allows the steam to escape and stops the crust from getting soggy! Making sweet pastry is very similar to making savory pastry, so read the recipe carefully and note the important differences!

The filling from the crisp on p.90-91 would taste great in this recipe.

Tools

- ❑ sieve
- ❑ 2 large mixing bowls
- ❑ fork
- ❑ table knife
- ❑ plastic wrap
- ❑ wooden spoon
- ❑ pie plate (approx. 9 in in diameter)
- ❑ rolling pin
- ❑ pastry brush
- ❑ oven mitts

Ingredients for 1 pie

1¾ cups flour

1 pinch table salt

½ cup unsalted butter (diced)

1 egg yolk (beaten with 1 Tbsp water)

2 Tbsp sugar

1 egg, beaten (for glazing)

For the filling

1½ lb apples (peeled, cored, and cut into wedges)

1 tsp vanilla extract

½ tsp ground cinnamon

½ cup soft light brown sugar

½ orange (zest and juice)

½ cup chopped walnuts (optional)

Recipe idea

Make sure you use apples that are suitable for cooking and eating, such as Cox's, Golden Delicious, or McIntosh.

Chef's tip
Use the excess pastry from Step 6 to make leaf shapes and decorate the pie. Put them on top of the pie before baking in Step 7.

1. **Sift** the flour and salt into the bowl and stir in the sugar. Using a fork, gently stir the diced butter into the flour until it is completely coated.

2. Using your fingertips, **rub** the butter into the flour until it looks like coarse breadcrumbs. See p.124 for expert tips on rubbing pastry.

3. Stir the water and egg yolk (drop by drop) into the crumbs with a table knife until they stick together in lumps. Gather the pastry in your hands.

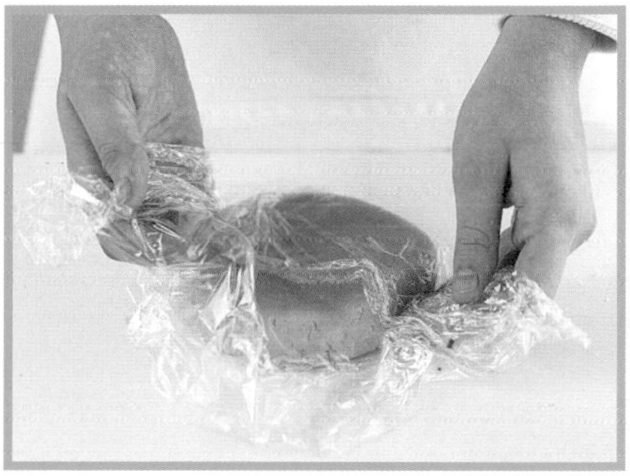

4. Put the pastry on a lightly-floured work surface and quickly shape into a smooth disc. Wrap the disc in plastic wrap and chill it for 1 hour, or until firm.

5. Preheat the oven to 425°F. Mix the sugar, cinnamon, vanilla extract, orange juice, orange zest, walnuts, and apples together in a bowl.

6. Pour the filling into the plate. Dampen the edge of the plate. **Roll** the pastry out to about ⅛ in thick and place it over the plate. Trim the excess.

7. Press the edges of the pastry into the plate and **crimp** with a fork. **Glaze** the pie with egg and make a hole in the center. Bake for 30–35 minutes, until golden.

Chocolate cake

When baking a cake, make sure that the oven is at the right temperature before you put the cake in. When the cake is in the oven, don't open the door to check on the cake until the cooking time has elapsed, otherwise it will sink!

For a flat top, put the second cake on upside down!

Tools

- ❑ electric mixer
- ❑ sieve
- ❑ large mixing bowl
- ❑ small mixing bowl
- ❑ serving spoon
- ❑ 2 8-in round cake pans, nonstick
- ❑ parchment paper
- ❑ small saucepan
- ❑ rubber spoon spatula
- ❑ oven mitts
- ❑ cooling rack
- ❑ palette knife
- ❑ serving plate

Ingredients for 1 cake

3 beaten eggs (at room temperature)

¾ cup unsalted butter (softened)

¾ cup sugar

½ tsp baking powder

1 ¼ cups self-rising flour

oil, for greasing

4 tsp cocoa powder

For the frosting

3½ oz milk chocolate

1 cup heavy cream (at room temperature)

3½ oz semisweet chocolate

Recipe idea

For a tasty frosting, melt ½ cup white chocolate (see Step 4) and pour into a wax paper-lined tray. Leave it to set. Break the set chocolate into small pieces and use it to decorate the top of the cake.

Food fact

The beaten eggs used in Step 1 should be at room temperature and added slowly, otherwise the cake mixture may curdle. If the mixture does start to curdle, mix in a little flour.

1. **Grease** the cake pans and **line** the bases. **Cream** the butter and sugar together in a bowl until they are light and fluffy. Gradually **beat** in the egg.

2. Preheat the oven to 350°F. **Sift** the flour, cocoa powder, and baking powder into the bowl and **fold** them into the creamed mixture.

3. Divide the mixture equally between the two greased and lined cake pans, smoothing the tops with a palette knife. Bake for 20–25 minutes or until firm.

4. Turn the cooked cakes out onto a cooling rack. Break both types of chocolate into a bowl and gently **melt** them over a pan of simmering water.

5. Remove the bowl from the pan. Allow the chocolate to cool for 5 minutes and then stir in the cream. Leave the mixture to thicken for a few minutes.

6. Make sure the cakes are completely cool before putting on the frosting. Put one cake on a serving plate and spread a quarter of the frosting over it.

7. Put the other cake on top and spoon on the rest of the frosting. Spread it over the top and the sides until the cake is evenly coated. Leave to set.

Tools

Here is a handy guide to all the equipment used in this book. Each recipe has a tool checklist so that you can gather everything you need before you begin cooking:

The basic tools

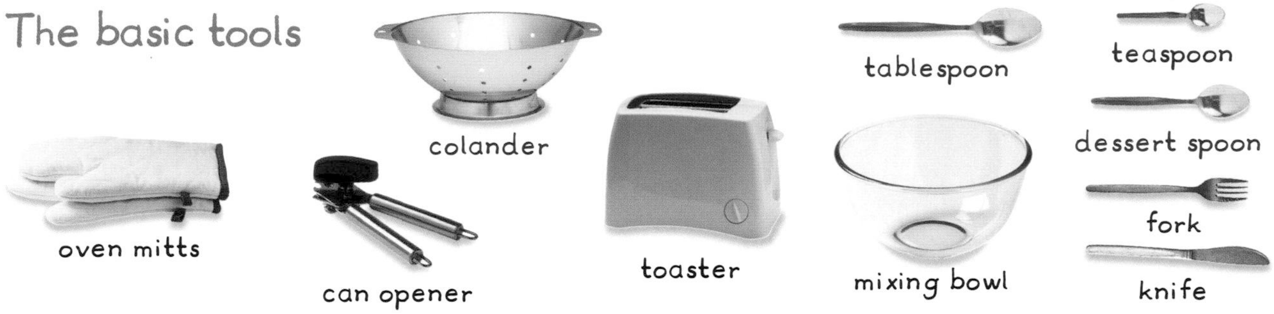

Baking tools

Crushing, juicing, and blending

Cutting and chopping

cook's knife

scissors

bread knife

carving knife

vegetable peeler

paring knife

utility knife

cutting board

grater

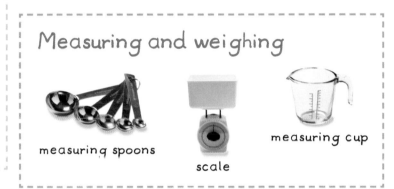

Spoons and spatulas

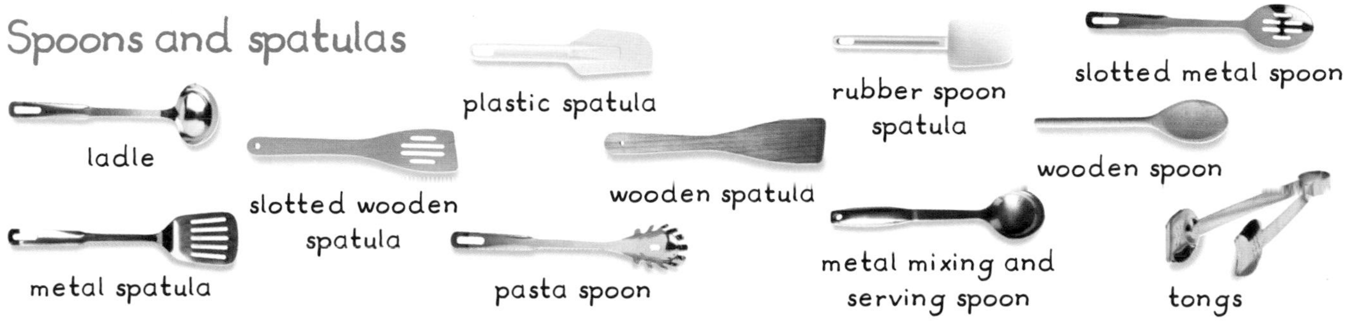

plastic spatula

rubber spoon spatula

slotted metal spoon

ladle

wooden spoon

slotted wooden spatula

wooden spatula

metal spatula

pasta spoon

metal mixing and serving spoon

tongs

Whisking

flat whisk

electric mixer

balloon whisk

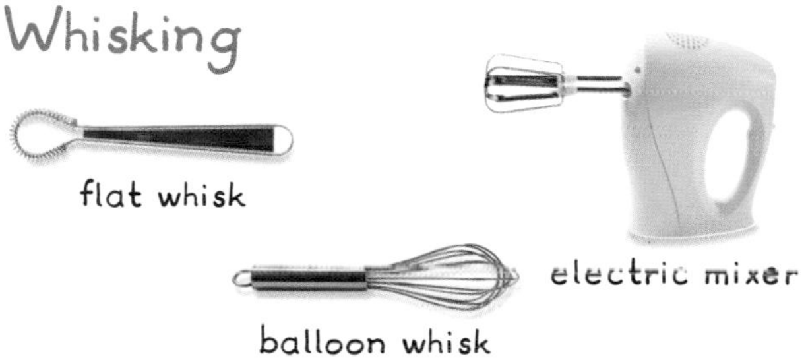

Measuring and weighing

measuring spoons

scale

measuring cup

Pots and pans

saucepan

frying pan

wok

sauté pan

grill pan

Miscellaneous tools

ovenproof dish

bamboo rolling mat

small ovenproof dish

pie plate

wooden kebab skewers

fruit-pop mold and sticks

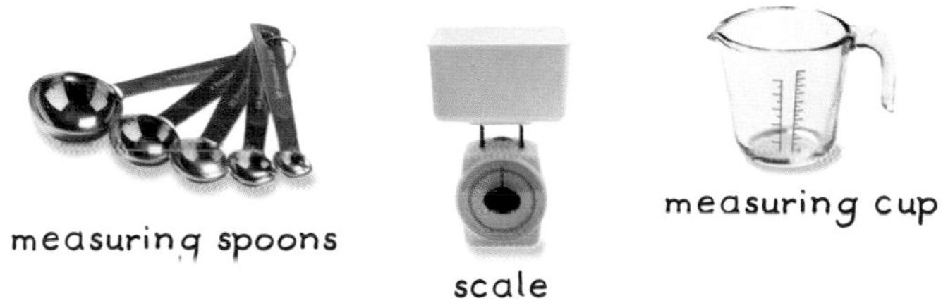

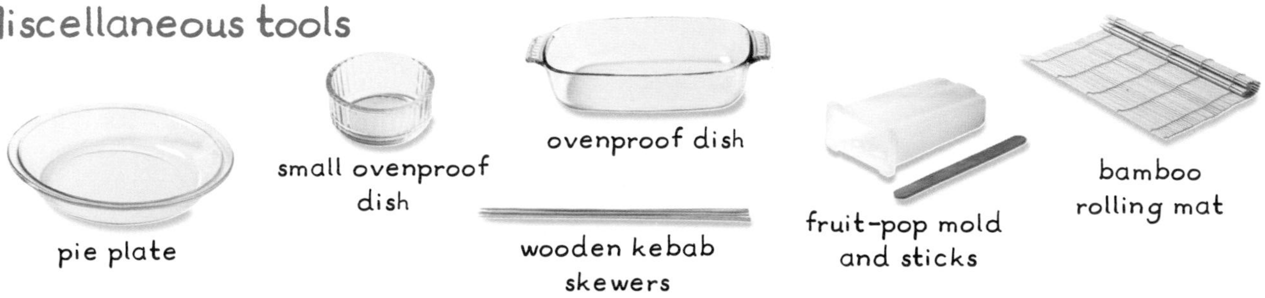

Glossary

This is the place to find extra information about the cooking terms and techniques used in this book. Key words are explained simply, plus there are chef's tips to give you even more handy hints.

Cutting words

Food is often cut into smaller pieces to make it easier to cook with and eat. Here are some cutting words:

Chopping—cutting into smaller pieces with a knife.
Coring—removing the core of a fruit. The core is the hard central part of some fruit, such as apples.
Crushing—breaking food up into very small pieces, e.g. with a garlic press.
Cubing—cutting into cubes of about 1 in square.
Deseeding—removing the seeds of fruit and vegetables, such as peppers, tomatoes, and cucumbers.
Dicing—cutting into small cubes.
Grating—rubbing food against a grater to make coarse or fine shreds.
Hulling—cutting off the green stalks and leaves of fruit, such as strawberries.
Juicing—squeezing the liquid from fruit or vegetables.
Mashing—crushing food, such as bananas or cooked potatoes, to make a smooth texture.
Peeling—removing the skin or outer layer of vegetables and fruit, by hand or with a knife. Some vegetables, such as onions and garlic, are always peeled before use.
Pitting—removing the large stone at the center of some fruit, such as peaches or mangoes.
Roughly chopping—cutting into pieces of varying sizes.
Scoring—making long, shallow cuts in food, to reduce cooking time or allow flavor to be absorbed.
Slicing—cutting food into thick or thin pieces.
Strips—long, thick or thin pieces.
Tailing—removing the stalk or tips of a vegetable.
Trimming—cutting off the unwanted parts of fruit, vegetables, meat, or fish.
Zesting—finely grating the rind of oranges, lemons, or limes to make zest, which is used as a flavoring.

★ Chef's tips

How to dice an onion

First cut the onion in half through the root and then peel off the skin. Place one half flat-side-down and firmly hold the onion so that the root is near your little finger. Carefully cut parallel slices, horizontally towards the root (Step 1). Turn the root of the onion away from you and slices downward from the root (Step 2). Turn the root back towards your little finger and slice across the onion so that it falls away in small cubes (Step 3). To chop an onion, just follow Steps 2 and 3.

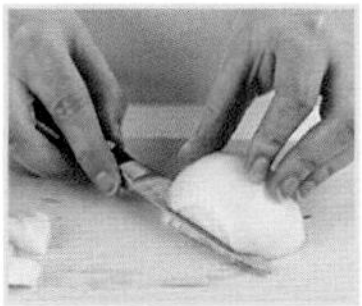

Step 1

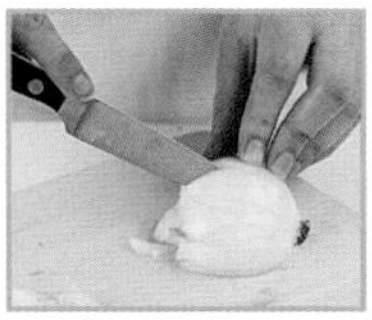

Step 2

Step 3

How to crush garlic

crushing garlic

Break open the garlic bulb and remove the cloves. Peel each clove and place them in a garlic press, one at a time. Squeeze the handle to crush the garlic and press it through the holes.

How to deseed a pepper

Cut the top off the pepper. Inside, you will see the core and the seeds. Carefully cut any parts attached to the side of the pepper and pull out the core and seeds.

deseeding

How to juice an orange

juicing

Cut an orange in half. Hold each half in turn over a bowl and press a reamer or juicer into the center. Twist the orange or reamer so that the juice drips into the bowl, and then remove any seeds.

Cooking words

Many of the recipes ask you to **preheat** the oven or broiler, which means to heat it to the correct temperature before you begin. This helps the food to cook thoroughly and evenly. Here are some other words to help you:

Baking—cooking food in an oven with dry heat (without any liquid). The outside will become brown.
Basting—spooning hot fat or a marinade over the food during cooking to keep it from drying out.
Boiling—when a liquid, such as water reaches boiling point it bubbles and is very hot.
Broiling—cooking or browning under an intense heat.
Dry-frying—frying without oil or fat.
Frying—cooking in a frying pan or saucepan with a little oil, over direct heat.
Parboiling—boiling for half the normal cooking time to soften, not completely cook.
Poaching—cooking in gently simmering liquid.
Reducing—simmering a liquid, such as a sauce, so that it thickens and reduces in quantity.
Roasting—cooking in the oven at a high temperature.
Sautéing—frying quickly in a little oil or fat.
Shallow-frying—frying in about ½ in or more of oil so that the outside turns golden and crispy.
Simmering—cooking over a low heat so the liquid or food is bubbling gently but not boiling.
Stir-frying—frying quickly in a little oil or fat over a high heat, stirring constantly.
Stove-top grilling—cooking or browning in a grill pan, on a stove.
Toasting—browning and crisping food under a broiler, in a toaster, or in the oven.
Warming—heating gently over a low heat, without boiling.

★ Chef's tips

How to roast a red pepper

Preheat the oven to 425°F. Brush a pepper with oil and place it on a baking tray. Roast for 30 minutes or until the skin starts to blacken. Allow the pepper to cool before peeling and deseeding it.

How to make sure meat is cooked

It is very important that you always make sure meat is cooked thoroughly. Although meat sometimes looks cooked on the outside, you should make sure the center is not pink or bloody. To check a roast chicken, stick a skewer into the center or thickest part of the meat. If the juices that run out are clear (not bloody or pink), then the meat is thoroughly cooked.

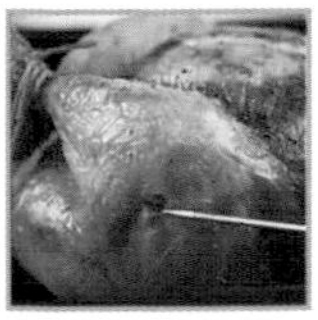
roast chicken

Mixing words

Mixing means putting ingredients together. There are lots of mixing words.

Beating—stirring or mixing quickly until smooth, to break down air.
Blending—mixing ingredients together using a blender, or food processor, to form a liquid or smooth mass.
Creaming—beating butter and sugar together to incorporate air.
Folding—a gentle way of mixing ingredients together, to retain as much air in the mixture as possible.
Whipping—beating ingredients, such as cream or egg whites, to add air and make them thicker.
Whisking—evenly mixing ingredients with a whisk or another word for whipping.

★ Chef's tips

How to beat an egg

To beat an egg, crack the egg into a bowl and stir vigorously with a fork or whisk.

beating

How to cream butter and sugar

creaming

Make sure the butter is soft (room temperature) and cut it into cubes. Whisk the butter and sugar together or beat with a wooden spoon to incorporate air and make a light and fluffy mixture.

How to fold ingredients

Use a metal spoon or plastic spatula to gently lift and turn the ingredients until they are just mixed together to avoid losing precious air from the mixture.

folding

whipping

How to whip cream

Use a hand whisk or electric mixer to vigorously whip the cream until it forms soft, firm peaks. Do not over-whip as this will make the cream curdle.

Bread-making

Bread-making is a lot of fun, but you'll need plenty of energy for all that kneading! Here are some useful bread-making terms:

Kneading—pressing and folding the dough with your hands until it is smooth and stretchy. This distributes the yeast and helps it to rise.
Proving—this is the correct name for the process of rising in bread-making.
Punching down—deflating the dough with a gentle punch. This evens out the texture of the bread.
Rising—the time it takes for the dough to increase in size.

★ Chef's tips

kneading

How to knead dough

Lightly sprinkle flour on the work surface and use one hand to hold the dough. With the heel of the other hand, gently push the dough away from you and then lift the dough back over. Repeat for about 10 minutes until the dough is smooth and stretchy, rotating frequently for even kneading.

punching down

How to punch down dough

After the dough has risen and doubled in size, it will need to be punched down. Press down firmly with your knuckles and the dough will deflate.

Pastry-making

Shortcrust pastry is the type usually used for pies or tarts. **Puff** pastry is light and flaky. Here are some useful pastry words:

Baking blind—weighing down a pastry base with baking beans to stop it from rising during baking.
Crimping—sealing or decorating the edges of pastry with a fork or by pinching with your fingers.
Glazing—brushing egg yolk or milk onto pastry (or dough) to make it look shiny when cooked.
Rolling—flattening the pastry with a rolling pin to make a bigger, thinner sheet.
Rubbing—mixing fat into the flour with your fingertips until it resembles breadcrumbs.

★ Chef's tips

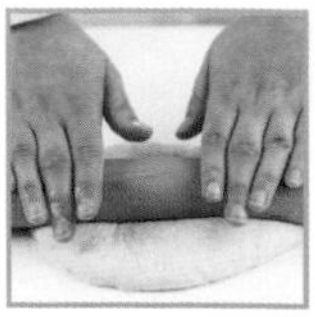
rolling pastry

How to roll pastry or dough

Sprinkle some flour onto the work surface and rolling pin. Roll the rolling pin across the pastry, away from you. Rotate the pastry and sprinkle more flour if needed. Keep rolling and rotating until you get the right shape and thickness. Always roll the pastry slightly bigger than you need.

baking blind

How to bake blind

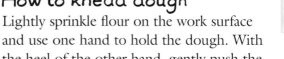

Cover the base of the pastry with a double layer of parchment paper and weigh it down with special baking beans or other dried beans. Bake blind for 15 minutes, or as directed in the recipe.

Cake-making

Here are some useful cake-making words:

Greasing—lightly coating the inside of a cake pan or other surface with oil or fat to prevent sticking.
Lining—covering a cake tin in parchment paper to prevent sticking.
Melting—heating a solid, such as chocolate or butter, to turn it into a liquid.
Sifting—putting a powdery ingredient, such as flour, through a sieve to remove lumps and aerate the mixture.

★ Chef's tips

How to grease and line a cake pan

lining

greasing

With a pencil, draw around the cake tin onto some parchment paper. Cut around the outline with scissors. Grease the tin by rubbing butter or oil all over the inside, using a small piece of parchment paper. Lay the parchment paper on the bottom of the tin.

How to tell if a cake is cooked

testing a cake

Insert a skewer or knife into the center of a cake. If it comes out clean (without any cake mixture), the cake is cooked; if the skewer comes out with mixture on it, bake for a few more minutes.

Egg words

All the recipes in this book use medium-sized eggs which should be at room temperature. The names for the parts of an egg are:

Shell—the hard outer covering of the egg.
White—the clear, runny part of the egg that turns white when cooked.
Yolk—the yellow ball in the center of the egg.

★ Chef's tips

How to check for freshness

fresh egg test

Most eggs have a "use-by date" on the carton, but here's a handy tip: place an egg in a glass of water—if it is fresh (good), the egg will lie horizontally on the bottom, but if it is stale (bad), it will stand upright and pop up to the top of the glass. You should never use a stale egg.

cracking an egg

How to crack an egg

Tap the egg firmly on the side of a bowl or cup, gently pull the sides apart, and let the insides drop into the container. It is best to crack an egg into a separate dish before adding it to your mixture, in case pieces of the shell fall in.

How to separate an egg

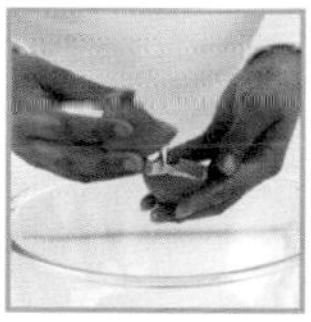

separating an egg white from the yolk

Crack the egg over a bowl and break it open gently. Don't let the yolk fall into the bowl—tip it carefully from one half of the shell to the other until all the white has dropped into the bowl. Put the yolk into a separate bowl.

Useful words

Here are some more words that you will learn in this book:

Absorb—to soak up, usually during cooking.
Batter—a runny mixture made of flour, eggs, and milk.
Caramelizing—turning brown and sticky when heated; this happens if the food has a sweet coating or sauce.
Chill—to cool in a refrigerator.
Coat—to cover with a layer of something, such as flour.
Curdle—when the liquid and solid parts of an ingredient or mixture separate. Milk curdles when over-heated and cakes can curdle if the eggs are too cold or added too quickly.
Dash—a small quantity.
Defrost—to thaw frozen food.
Dollop—a large spoonful of a soft food.
Drain—to remove unwanted liquid, sometimes with a colander or sieve.
Drizzle—to pour slowly, in a trickle.
Drop—a single splash of liquid.
Freeze—to turn a liquid into a solid by storing it in an extremely cold place (freezer).
Marinade—a mixture of oil, herbs, spices, and other seasonings in which food is soaked to add flavor.
Marinate—to soak meat, fish, or vegetables in a marinade to add flavour or tenderize.
Paste—a soft, thick mixture.
Pat—a small lump of a solid ingredient, such as butter.
Pinch—as much of a powdery ingredient as you can hold between your finger and thumb.
Prick—to make small holes in something.
Purée—a thick pulp produced by blending or sieving.
Refresh—to rinse a just-cooked food in cold water to prevent further cooking.
Rest—to set aside food for a short time, usually to allow a change in texture, as with roasted meat.
Rind—the hard outer edge of cheese or fruit.
Rinse—to wash in running water from the faucet.
Ripe—when a fruit is soft and ready to be eaten.
Scatter—to roughly sprinkle pieces of an ingredient or food over something with your hands.
Seal—to close up or encase a food to prevent anything from getting in or out.
Season—to add salt and pepper to a food to balance and enhance its natural flavor.
Set—to turn from a liquid into a solid.
Shape—to use your hands to turn a soft food or mixture into a particular shape.
Sift—to use a sieve to remove lumps from a dry ingredient.
Sprinkle—to scatter a food lightly over something.
Stand—to set a food aside for a while to cool, finish cooking, or improve the flavor.
Stock—a flavored liquid in which meat, fish, or vegetables are cooked.
Strain—to use a sieve to drain a liquid.
Thicken—to add an ingredient, such as flour, to make a liquid less thin.
Wedges—thick pieces with a pointed or thin edge.

Index